" . . . I think we at least have to examine the proposition that there's such a thing as knowing more than is good for us . . . "

Dan Dennett

" . . . Whether it's astrology or religion or anything else, I want to live in a world where people think sceptically for themselves, look at evidence . . . "

Richard Dawkins

" . . . I think there's a place for the sacred in our lives, but under some construal that doesn't presuppose any bullshit . . . "

Sam Harris

" . . . We don't desecrate. We would, for the reasons given by Sophocles in *Antigone*, have a natural resistance to profanity and desecration. We leave it to the pious to destroy churches and burn synagogues or blow up each other's mosques . . . "

Christopher Hitchens

THE FOUR HORSEMEN

DAWKINS

FOREWORD BY STEPHEN FRY

DENNETT

THE FOUR HORSEMEN

HARRIS

THE DISCUSSION THAT SPARKED
AN ATHEIST REVOLUTION

HITCHENS

BANTAM PRESS

TRANSWORLD PUBLISHERS
61–63 Uxbridge Road, London W5 5SA
www.penguin.co.uk

Transworld is part of the Penguin Random House group of companies
whose addresses can be found at global.penguinrandomhouse.com

First published in Great Britain in 2019 by Bantam Press
an imprint of Transworld Publishers

A CIP catalogue record for this book is available from the British Library.

ISBN 9780593080399

Typeset in 12.5/16.5pt Bulmer MT Std by Jouve (UK), Milton Keynes
Printed and bound in Great Britain by Clays Ltd, Elcograf S.p.A.

Penguin Random House is committed to a sustainable
future for our business, our readers and our planet. This book
is made from Forest Stewardship Council® certified paper.

7 9 10 8

For Hitch

CONTENTS

FOREWORD
STEPHEN FRY

'*Do you believe in God?*'

'A question of little value. Which god? Ganesh? Osiris? Jove? Jehovah? Or one of the tens of thousands of animist gods worshipped every day around the globe?'

'Oh, very well then, if you're going to get clever – *any* god.'

'Do I believe in "any god"?'

'Look, there's a creation, isn't there? Therefore there must be a Creator. Nothing comes from nothing. Something must have started it all.'

'I'll overlook your reckless use of "therefore" and go along with you, out of interest. Just to see where it gets us.'

'Well then.'

'Well then, what?'

'You've agreed there's a Creator.'

'Well, I haven't *agreed*, but I've come along with you to see where it's going. Who *is* this Creator you have conjured up on the grounds that they "must" exist?'

'Well, we can't say.'

'And more important, who created this Creator?'

'That's just silly.'

'But you've just told me that nothing comes from nothing and that something must have started it all. Why am I not allowed to use this principle to wonder where your Creator comes from?'

'Well, you must admit that Love and Beauty can't be explained by science. That there's something other . . .'

We have all had heated, sophomoric and ultimately futile conversations like this as students – quibbling and quarrelling earnestly about turtles-all-the-way-down regress and challenging each other to prove the unprovable, long into the wine-fuelled night. We have all listened to those of faith stating their position, first by adducing half-understood scientific thinking and discovery—

'Quantum physics itself shows that we can't be certain of anything.'

—then dropping them contemptuously:

'Science doesn't have all the answers. It can't even explain what most of the universe is made of! Anyway, they're only theories.'

To this day, the 'No *true* Scotsman' fallacy is alive and well:

> 'Buddhism has a lot to teach us, you know. It's been shown to have real psychological and cognitive value.'
>
> 'You mean like those Buddhist monks who helped the Burmese army ethnically cleanse the Rohingya to the point of genocide?'
>
> 'Oh, but they weren't proper Buddhists.'

Such scenes play out every day, and it is important that they should. The rounds of punch and counterpunch may get wearisome, aggressive and tiresomely circular, but let us never forget that this is a big subject and the claims made by theists, religionists and believers are the most momentous claims there can be. About anything. You don't have to boast a PhD or have read Thomas à Kempis, the Qur'an, the Book of Mormon and the teachings of Siddhartha (or indeed *On the Origin of Species* and *Principia Mathematica*) to be able to take part in such wrangling and disputation. But boy, isn't it wonderful when you can eavesdrop on four who *have*. It warms the heart, tickles the soul and fires up the synapses. And that is exactly what this book allows us to do – listen in on four people who have thought hard and fought hard (for they have been publicly battered and battled like few intellectuals in our time) without losing their wit, humour and sense of proportion.

So who are they, these Four Musketeers of the Mind? What do they want with us and the world? Why should we care?

Let us meet them one by one.

SAM HARRIS (Aramis) is a neuroscientist, moralist, author and enthusiastic exponent of Brazilian jiu-jitsu (a martial art most noted, I am told, for its close grappling and ferocious ground fighting). He is equally trained and proficient in forms of meditation that an Englishman of my caste finds incomprehensible and deeply embarrassing. I can't even say the word 'mindfulness' without blushing. Harris's influential books *The End of Faith* and *Letter to a Christian Nation* were followed by a later book and subsequent highly popular podcast series called *Waking Up*, which focus on his great interest in exploring how morality and spirituality can flourish outside religious teaching.

DANIEL DENNETT (Athos) is a philosopher. Perhaps the best-known philosopher alive. A few years ago, that would have been like calling someone the best-known fluid dynamicist alive or the most famous coleopterist the world has ever seen, but these days philosophy and its branches are *hot*. More people are choosing it as an undergraduate subject, it seems, than ever before. As a UC

Berkeley alumni magazine headline neatly phrased it, 'Philosophy's Popularity Soars: Devotees Find It's More Than "An Interesting Path to Poverty"'. Professor Dennett writes on the mind, evolutionary biology, free will and much else besides. His book *Breaking the Spell: Religion as a Natural Phenomenon* caused plenty of fluttering in academic, intellectual, religious and political dovecots. His co-authorship with Asbjørn Steglich-Petersen of *The Philosophical Lexicon* has alone guaranteed him eternal glory. Like Einstein, Noah and the Kennedys, Professor Dennett is a keen sailor.

RICHARD DAWKINS (d'Artagnan) is responsible for introducing evolutionary biology and Darwinism to generations. His books *The Selfish Gene* and *The Blind Watchmaker*, never out of print, continue to inspire, inform and amaze. As the first holder of Oxford University's Simonyi Professorship for the Public Understanding of Science, he acquired a worldwide reputation as a sceptic, 'passionate rationalist', 'proud atheist', and witty exposer of charlatanism and fakery couched in pseudo-scientific language. In all that time, he has pursued an academic career as a leading ethologist and biologist. He gave our language the word 'meme', and in his work as a scientist has hugely expanded our understanding not just of the genotype but of the whole evolutionary package that makes life, the phenotype. His Richard Dawkins

Foundation for Reason and Science stands as a global cynosure for free thought.

CHRISTOPHER HITCHENS (Porthos) was – and how it will always grieve me to have to use the past tense – a journalist, essayist, polemicist, contrarian, debater, political historian, author and thinker. His preternaturally fluent articulacy, breadth of learning, extraordinary recall, diablerie, sauciness, and panache raised his mastery of debate to a level unmatched in his lifetime. We are fortunate that this child of the 1960s and '70s did at least make it into the YouTube era; many of his coruscating flagellations of the dim-witted, malevolent, ill-informed and unprepared live on in cyberspace as well as in the pages of his many articles, essays and books.

Richard Dawkins sets the context of this meeting of the Horsemen very well indeed in his new contribution to this book, but it is worth recalling how the Four had, between them, broken new ground in the English-speaking world, opening up debate everywhere, empowering humanism and secularism for a new generation, and giving voice to the always lurking and now growing suspicion that the worst aspects of religion, from faith-healing fakery to murderous martyrdom, could not be separated from the essential nature of religion itself. They did so with the publication of enormously influential books: Harris's *The End of Faith*, Dawkins's *The God Delusion*, Dennett's *Breaking the Spell* and Hitchens's *God Is Not Great*. These appeared against a millennial background of growing Christian evangelical fundamentalism in the United States and murderous jihadism in the Islamic world.

The emperor had been parading about for centuries, and it was time someone pointed and reminded the world that he was naked. The response was, as might be imagined, intense. The four became media stars to the extent that they were asked to comment and debate at all times and in all places. But a counter-reformation followed. Religionists of all stripes, most of whom appeared not to have read the books,[1] fought back against these new voices:

'The New Atheism is just like a religion.'

'These New Atheists are fundamentalists themselves.'

'How dare they affront and wound people for whom religion is so great a solace, balm, and support?'

'Lenin and Stalin imposed atheism in the USSR, and look where that led.'

'They define all of us according to the behaviour of the worst of us.'

---

[1] Compare and contrast with the Four Horsemen, whose breadth of scriptural and theological knowledge is impressively on display in the pages to come.

Such accusations – which are assertions, of course, not arguments, with their resentful air of noble hurt – were brandished as if they constituted a refutation of all that this New Atheism stood for. After thousands of years of supremacy, suppression and censorship, the champions of religion managed to transform themselves miraculously into victims of cruel verbal abuse, snobbish bullying and intellectual persecution. It is against such a background that this conversation takes place.

Indeed, the first topic that Dawkins, Dennett, Harris and Hitchens address is that very issue of 'offence' – how offence is taken by religion's guardians whenever their claims and practices are examined in the forensic light of reason, history and knowledge. Reading the Four Horsemen on this subject now, one realizes that all conversations about any ideology or belief are subsets of the religious debate. Questions of free speech, blasphemy, sacrilege and heresy have a sharp relevance in our far-from-brave new world of culture wars, denunciation, shaming, no-platforming, and the pestilential swarm of Year Zero ills that has flown chattering, stinging and biting from the Pandora's Box of social media.

Yes, the Four Horsemen can be mordant and almost cruel in their swatting of adversarial flies, but they always play by the rules. The rules of all intellectual activity – whether scientific or non-scientific – spin down to one golden precept: the testing of assertions on the anvils of logic and verifiable fact. For an argument to obtain, it must make sense rationally and empirically.

This does not cast the New Atheist as a cold, unfeeling Mr Spock. Reason and experience recognize that many pious adherents are sincere in their faith. While it is honourable and legitimate to speculate as to the truth of the tenets of religious faith, there is no call to mock or undermine the individually devout. Flaubert's *Coeur simple*, the old servant Félicité on her knees, telling the rosary and looking up with reverent wonder at the stained-glass window above the altar, is not ripe for scorn; but the dogma relayed from the Vatican by the cardinal in his palace, dogma that keeps Félicité on her knees, the palace stocked with wine, and the populace plied with nonsensical edicts and eschatological threats . . . well, that is fair and necessary game. Enquiries into the legitimacy of claims that spill out into the public arena and influence education, law-making and policy have no obligation to consider bruised feelings.

If the truth of the existence of God is a first-order matter, it is soon dropped in debates and replaced with second-order questions:

> Maybe faith and belief in divinity and an afterlife, even if founded on claims for which there can be no evidence, may nonetheless be considered a force for good?

Maybe they offer moral guides and ethical codes without which the world would be a cruel and riotous place? Much of what we live by is metaphor. Why shouldn't we accept a religious narrative irrespective of its truth – as a framework in this relativist culture cursed by the disappearance of structure, hierarchy, and meaning?

And what about the spiritual, the numinous immanence we all feel? Can you really deny that there is a realm which reason and numbers and microscopes cannot penetrate?

The Fearless Four dive right into all these second-order topics. While not going so far as to allow for Stephen Jay Gould's unsatisfactory proposition of NOMA (Non-Overlapping Magisteria, an idea that can be expressed as 'Render unto science what is science's, and render unto religion all the rest'), we can see that each member of the Four is happy to agree that the world, the cosmos, and our human apprehension exhibit and experience the numinous. This is not any kind of concession, for *numen* is (despite what some dictionaries might suggest) no more suggestive of the existence of divinity than *lumen*, or indeed any less attractive phenomena – cruelty, cancer and flesh-eating bacteria, for example.

The glory of this gathering is that everything each player in the quartet contributes on religion and atheism, science and sense, applies with equal urgency to the troublesome topics of our present age. Sitting in on these dialogues of Dawkins, Harris, Dennett and Hitchens reminds us that open enquiry, free thinking and the unfettered exchange of ideas yield real and tangible fruit. Who imagined that the future of such obvious and surely ineluctable enlightenment principles might in our life-time be threatened – threatened by shrieking intolerance from both sides of the old political divide, but also by our own fear, indolence and misplaced courtesy? This real danger is what makes the publication of this book so timely and welcome. May new generations continue to be inspired by the glamour and glory of the Four, and the valour and value of free thought openly and gracefully exchanged.

One for all, and all for one!

THE HUBRIS OF RELIGION, THE HUMILITY OF SCIENCE, AND THE INTELLECTUAL AND MORAL COURAGE OF ATHEISM

RICHARD DAWKINS

Between 2004 and 2007, five bestselling books became known – notorious, in some circles – as the spearhead of a so-called New Atheist movement. They were Sam Harris's *The End of Faith* (2004) and *Letter to a Christian Nation* (2006), Daniel Dennett's *Breaking the Spell* (2006), my *The God Delusion* (2006) and Christopher Hitchens's *God Is Not Great* (2007). For a time, Sam, Dan and I were dubbed 'the Three Musketeers'. Then, when Christopher's broadside arrived, we expanded into 'the Four Horsemen'. We were not responsible for those journalistic coinings but we didn't disown them. Nor did we collude with each other: there was no organized mustering of the guns, although we had no objection to being bracketed together, and we were happy to be joined by such respected authors as Ayaan Hirsi Ali, Victor Stenger, Lawrence Krauss, Jerry Coyne, Michael Shermer, A. C. Grayling and Dan Barker, among others.

In September 2007, the annual conference of the Atheist Alliance International was held in Washington DC, Christopher Hitchens's home city. Robin Elisabeth Cornwell, on behalf of the Richard Dawkins Foundation for Reason and Science, took advantage of the presence of all four 'horsemen' in the same place and organized a joint conversation, to be filmed by our resident cinematographers. The plan was that Ayaan Hirsi Ali would make a fifth, as lone horsewoman, thereby taking our progression on from Three Musketeers through Four Horsemen to Five Pillars of Wisdom. At the last minute, Ayaan unfortunately had to make an emergency dash to the Netherlands, where she had been a Member of Parliament. We missed her, and were pleased that she joined the three surviving horsemen in 2012, when the Global Atheist Convention in Melbourne staged a form of reprise.[1] Her presence unsurprisingly stimulated a partial switch to Islam as a topic.

Now, back to the original meeting in 2007. In the evening of 30 September, the four of us sat round a table in

[1] https://www.youtube.com/watch?v=sOMjEJ3JO5Q.

Christopher and Carol's airy, book-lined flat. Plied with cocktails, we had a two-hour conversation followed by a memorable dinner. The film of our discussion was made available on the YouTube channel of the Richard Dawkins Foundation.[1] The foundation also launched the recording as a pair of DVDs; the text that follows in this book is a transcript of our conversation.

For me, the event was a vindication of my conviction that discussion doesn't always need a chairman or any basic disagreement or debate to maintain interest and bear fruit. We didn't even have a prepared agenda. The conversation took its own course. Yet nobody hogged the floor, and we segued seamlessly over a great number of topics. The two hours seemed to fly by, and our own interest never flagged. Does the unsteered conversation remain interesting to a third party? That is for readers of this book to judge.

How different would our conversation be if we had it today, a decade or so later? It's impossible to overlook the obvious difference: no Christopher Hitchens, our gracious host on that memorable evening. How we would miss – do miss – that strong, mellifluous baritone, the prodigious learning, the erudite quotations from literature and history, the barbed yet gentlemanly wit, the eloquent cadences impelled forward by such rhetorical skills as

---

[1] https://www.youtube.com/watch?v=n7IHU28aR2E.

the dramatic pause *after* rather than before the first word of a new sentence. I won't say he dominated our four-way conversation, but he certainly had a decisive effect on the flow of it.

Rather than rehearse old themes, I thought I'd use this essay to develop new points that I might make if we were to have another such discussion today.

❖

Among the many topics we discussed in 2007 was how religion and science compared in respect of humility and hubris. Religion, for its part, stands accused of conspicuous overconfidence and sensational lack of humility. The expanding universe, the laws of physics, the fine-tuned physical constants, the laws of chemistry, the slow grind of evolution's mills – all were set in motion so that, in the 14-billion-year fullness of time, we should come into existence. Even the constantly reiterated insistence that we are miserable offenders, born in sin, is a kind of inverted arrogance: such vanity, to presume that our moral conduct has some sort of cosmic significance, as though the Creator of the Universe wouldn't have better things to do than tot up our black marks and our brownie points. The universe is all concerned with me. Is that not the arrogance that passeth all understanding?

Carl Sagan, in *Pale Blue Dot*,[1] makes the exculpatory point that our distant ancestors could scarcely escape such cosmic narcissism. With no roof over their heads and no artificial light, they nightly watched the stars wheeling overhead. And what was at the centre of the wheel? The exact location of the observer, of course. No wonder they thought the universe was 'all about me'. In the other sense of 'about', it did indeed revolve 'about me'. 'I' was the epicentre of the cosmos. But that excuse, if it is one, evaporated with Copernicus and Galileo.

Turning, then, to theologians' overconfidence, admittedly few quite reach the heights scaled by the seventeenth-century archbishop James Ussher, who was so sure of his biblical chronology that he gave the origin of the universe a precise date: 22 October, 4004 BC. Not 21 or 23 October but precisely on the evening of 22 October. Not September or November but definitely, with the immense authority of the Church, October. Not 4003 or 4005, not 'somewhere around the fourth or fifth millennium BC' but, no doubt about it, 4004 BC. Others, as I said, are not quite so precise about it, but it is characteristic of theologians that they just make stuff up. Make it up with liberal abandon and force it, with a presumed

[1] Carl Sagan, *Pale Blue Dot: A Vision of the Human Future in Space* (New York: Random House, 1994).

limitless authority, upon others, sometimes – at least in former times and still today in Islamic theocracies – on pain of torture and death.

Such arbitrary precision shows itself, too, in the bossy rules for living that religious leaders impose on their followers. And when it comes to control-freakery, Islam is way out ahead, in a class of its own. Here are some choice examples from the *Concise Commandments of Islam* handed down by Ayatollah Ozma Sayyed Mohammad Reda Musavi Golpaygani, a respected Iranian 'scholar'. Concerning the wet-nursing of babies, alone, there are no fewer than twenty-three minutely specified rules, translated as 'Issues'. Here's the first of them, Issue 547. The rest are equally precise, equally bossy, and equally devoid of apparent rationale:

> If a woman wet-nurses a child, in accordance to the conditions to be stated in Issue 560, the father of that child cannot marry the woman's daughters, nor can he marry the daughters of the husband whom the milk belongs to, even his wet-nurse daughters, but it is permissible for him to marry the wet-nurse daughters of the woman . . . [and it goes on].

Here's another example from the wet-nursing department, Issue 553:

> If the wife of a man's father wet-nurses a girl with his father's milk, then the man cannot marry that girl.

'*Father's* milk'? What? I suppose in a culture where a woman is the property of her husband, 'father's milk' is not as weird as it sounds to us.

Issue 555 is similarly puzzling, this time about 'brother's milk':

> A man cannot marry a girl who has been wet-nursed by his sister or his brother's wife with his brother's milk.

I don't know the origin of this creepy obsession with wet-nursing, but it is not without its scriptural basis:

> When the Qur'aan was first revealed, the number of breast-feedings that would make a child a relative (mah-ram) was ten, then this was abrogated and replaced with the number of five which is well-known.[1]

That was part of the reply from another 'scholar' to the following recent *cri de coeur* from a (pardonably) confused woman on social media:

> I breastfed my brother-in-law's son for a month, and my son was breastfed by my brother-in-law's wife. I have a daughter and a son who are older than the child who was breastfed by my brother-in-law's wife, and she also had two children before the child of hers whom I breastfed.

---

[1] https://islamqa.info/en/27280.

I hope that you can describe the kind of breastfeeding that makes the child a mahram and the rulings that apply to the rest of the siblings? Thank you very much.

The precision of 'five' breast feedings is typical of this kind of religious control-freakery. It surfaced bizarrely in a 2007 *fatwa* issued by Dr Izzat Atiyya, a lecturer at Al-Azhar University in Cairo, who was concerned about the prohibition against male and female colleagues being alone together and came up with an ingenious solution. The female colleague should feed her male colleague 'directly from her breast' at least five times. This would make them 'relatives' and thereby enable them to be alone together at work. Note that four times would not suffice. He apparently wasn't joking at the time, although he did retract his *fatwa* after the outcry it provoked. How can people bear to live their lives bound by such insanely specific yet manifestly pointless rules?

With some relief, perhaps, we turn to science. Science is often accused of arrogantly claiming to know everything, but the barb is capaciously wide of the mark. Scientists love not knowing the answer, because it gives us something to do, something to think about. We loudly assert ignorance, in a gleeful proclamation of what needs to be done.

How did life begin? I don't know, nobody knows, we wish we did, and we eagerly exchange hypotheses, together with suggestions for how to investigate them. What caused the apocalyptic mass extinction at the end of the Permian period, a quarter of a billion years ago? We don't know, but we have some interesting hypotheses to think about. What did the common ancestor of humans and chimpanzees look like? We don't know, but we do know a bit about it. We know the continent on which it lived (Africa, as Darwin guessed), and molecular evidence tells us roughly when (between 6 million and 8 million years ago). What is dark matter? We don't know, and a substantial fraction of the physics community would dearly like to.

Ignorance, to a scientist, is an itch that begs to be pleasurably scratched. Ignorance, if you are a theologian, is something to be washed away by shamelessly making something up. If you are an authority figure like the Pope, you might do it by thinking privately to yourself and waiting for an answer to pop into your head – which you then proclaim as a 'revelation'. Or you might do it by 'interpreting' a Bronze Age text whose author was even more ignorant than you are.

Popes can promulgate their private opinions as 'dogma', but only if those opinions have the backing of a substantial number of Catholics through history: long tradition of belief in a proposition is, somewhat mysteriously to a scientific mind, regarded as evidence for the truth of that proposition. In 1950, Pope Pius XII (unkindly known as

'Hitler's Pope') promulgated the dogma that Jesus' mother Mary, on her death, was bodily – i.e. not merely spiritually – lifted up into heaven. 'Bodily' means that if you'd looked in her grave, you'd have found it empty. The Pope's reasoning had absolutely nothing to do with evidence. He cited 1 Corinthians 15:54: 'then shall be brought to pass the saying that is written, Death is swallowed up in victory'. The saying makes no mention of Mary. There is not the smallest reason to suppose the author of the epistle had Mary in mind. We see again the typical theological trick of taking a text and 'interpreting' it in a way that just might have some vague, symbolic, hand-waving connection with something else. Presumably, too, like so many religious beliefs, Pius XII's dogma was at least partly based on a feeling of what would be *fitting* for one so holy as Mary. But the Pope's main motivation, according to Dr Kenneth Howell, director of the John Henry Cardinal Newman Institute of Catholic Thought, University of Illinois, came from a different meaning of what was fitting. The world of 1950 was recovering from the devastation of the Second World War and desperately needed the balm of a healing message. Howell quotes the Pope's words, then gives his own interpretation:

> Pius XII clearly expresses his hope that meditation on Mary's assumption will lead the faithful to a greater

awareness of our common dignity as the human family . . . What would impel human beings to keep their eyes fixed on their supernatural end and to desire the salvation of their fellow human beings? Mary's assumption was a reminder of, and impetus toward, greater respect for humanity because the Assumption cannot be separated from the rest of Mary's earthly life.

It's fascinating to see how the theological mind works: in particular, the lack of interest in – indeed, the contempt for – factual evidence. Never mind whether there's any evidence that Mary was assumed bodily into heaven; it would be good for people to believe she was. It isn't that theologians deliberately tell untruths. It's as though they just don't care about truth; aren't interested in truth; don't know what truth even means; demote truth to negligible status compared with other considerations, such as symbolic or mythic significance. And yet at the same time, Catholics are compelled to believe these made-up 'truths' – compelled in no uncertain terms. Even before Pius XII promulgated the Assumption as a dogma, the eighteenth-century Pope Benedict XIV declared the Assumption of Mary to be 'a probable opinion which to deny were impious and blasphemous'. If to deny a 'probable opinion' is 'impious and blasphemous', you can imagine the penalty for denying an infallible dogma!

Once again, note the brazen confidence with which religious leaders assert 'facts' which even they admit are supported by no historical evidence at all.

The *Catholic Encyclopedia* is a treasury of overconfident sophistry. Purgatory is a sort of celestial waiting room in which the dead are punished for their sins ('purged') before eventually being admitted to heaven. The *Encyclopedia*'s entry on purgatory has a long section on 'Errors', listing the mistaken views of heretics such as the Albigenses, Waldenses, Hussites and Apostolici, unsurprisingly joined by Martin Luther and John Calvin.[1]

The biblical evidence for the existence of purgatory is, shall we say, 'creative', again employing the common theological trick of vague, hand-waving analogy. For example, the *Encyclopedia* notes that 'God forgave the incredulity of Moses and Aaron, but as punishment kept them from the "land of promise"'. That banishment is viewed as a kind of metaphor for purgatory. More gruesomely, when David had Uriah the Hittite killed so that he could marry Uriah's beautiful wife, the Lord forgave him – but didn't let him off scot-free: God killed the child of the marriage (2 Samuel 12:13–14). Hard on the innocent child, you might think. But apparently a useful metaphor for the partial punishment that is purgatory, and one not overlooked by the *Encyclopedia*'s authors.

---

[1] http://www.catholic.org/encyclopedia/view.php?id=9745.

The section of the purgatory entry called 'Proofs' is interesting because it purports to use a form of logic. Here's how the argument goes. If the dead went straight to heaven, there'd be no point in our praying for their souls. And we do pray for their souls, don't we? Therefore it must follow that they don't go straight to heaven. Therefore there must be purgatory. QED. Are professors of theology really paid to do this kind of thing?

Enough; let's turn again to science. Scientists know when they don't know the answer. But they also know when they do, and they shouldn't be coy about proclaiming it. It's not hubristic to state known facts when the evidence is secure. Yes, yes, philosophers of science tell us a fact is no more than a hypothesis which may one day be falsified but which has so far withstood strenuous attempts to do so. Let us by all means pay lip service to that incantation, while muttering, in homage to Galileo's muttered *eppur si muove*, the sensible words of Stephen Jay Gould:

> In science, 'fact' can only mean 'confirmed to such a degree that it would be perverse to withhold provisional assent.' I suppose that apples might start to rise tomorrow, but the possibility does not merit equal time in physics classrooms.[1]

---

[1] Stephen Jay Gould, 'Evolution as fact and theory', in *Hen's Teeth and Horse's Toes* (New York: W. W. Norton, 1994).

Facts in this sense include the following, and not one of them owes anything whatsoever to the many millions of hours devoted to theological ratiocination. The universe began between 13 billion and 14 billion years ago. The sun, and the planets orbiting it, including ours, condensed out of a rotating disk of gas, dust and debris about 4.5 billion years ago. The map of the world changes as the tens of millions of years go by. We know the approximate shape of the continents and where they were at any named time in geological history. And we can project ahead and draw the map of the world as it will change in the future. We know how different the constellations in the sky would have appeared to our ancestors and how they will appear to our descendants.

Matter in the universe is non-randomly distributed in discrete bodies, many of them rotating, each on its own axis, and many of them in elliptical orbit around other such bodies according to mathematical laws which enable us to predict, to the exact second, when notable events such as eclipses and transits will occur. These bodies – stars, planets, planetesimals, knobbly chunks of rock, etc. – are themselves clustered in galaxies, many billions of them, separated by distances orders of magnitude larger than the (already very large) spacing of (again, many billions of) stars within galaxies.

Matter is composed of atoms, and there is a finite number of types of atoms – the hundred or so elements. We know the mass of each of these elemental atoms, and we know why any one element can have more than one iso-tope with slightly different mass. Chemists have a huge body of knowledge about how and why the elements combine in molecules. In living cells, molecules can be extremely large, constructed of thousands of atoms in precise, and exactly known, spatial relation to one another. The methods by which the exact structures of these macromolecules are discovered are wonderfully ingenious, involving meticulous measurements on the scattering of X-rays beamed through crystals. Among the macromolecules fathomed by this method is DNA, the universal genetic molecule. The strictly digital code by which DNA influences the shape and nature of proteins – another family of macromolecules which are the elegantly honed machine-tools of life – is exactly known in every detail. The ways in which those proteins influence the behaviour of cells in developing embryos, and hence influence the form and functioning of all living things, is work in progress: a great deal is known; much challeng-ingly remains to be learned.

For any particular gene in any individual animal, we can write down the exact sequence of DNA code letters in the gene. This means we can count, with total preci-sion, the number of single-letter discrepancies between two individuals. This is a serviceable measure of how long ago their common ancestor lived. This works for comparisons within a species – between you and Barack Obama, for instance. And it works for comparisons of different species – between you and an aardvark, say. Again, you can count the discrepancies exactly. There are just more discrepancies the further back in time the shared ancestor lived. Such precision lifts the spirit and justifies pride in our species, *Homo sapiens*. For once, and without hubris, Linnaeus's specific name seems warranted.

Hubris is unjustified pride. Pride can be justified, and science does so in spades. So does Beethoven, so do Shakespeare, Michelangelo, Christopher Wren. So do the engineers who built the giant telescopes in Hawaii and in the Canary Islands, the giant radio telescopes and very large arrays that stare sightless into the southern sky; or the Hubble orbiting telescope and the spacecraft that launched it. The engineering feats deep underground at CERN, combining monumental size with minutely accurate tolerances of measurement, literally moved me to tears when I was shown around. The engineering, the mathematics, the physics, in the Rosetta mission that successfully soft-landed a robot vehicle on the tiny target of a comet also made me proud to be human. Modified versions of the same technology may one day save our planet by enabling us to divert a dangerous comet like the one that killed the dinosaurs.

Who does not feel a swelling of human pride when

they hear about the LIGO instruments which, synchronously in Louisiana and Washington State, detected gravitation waves whose amplitude would be dwarfed by a single proton? This feat of measurement, with its profound significance for cosmology, is equivalent to measuring the distance from Earth to the star Proxima Centauri to an accuracy of one human hair's breadth.

Comparable accuracy is achieved in experimental tests of quantum theory. And here there is a revealing mismatch between our human capacity to demonstrate, with invincible conviction, the predictions of a theory experimentally and our capacity to visualize the theory itself. Our brains evolved to understand the movement of buffalo-sized objects at lion speeds in the moderately scaled spaces afforded by the African savanna. Evolution didn't equip us to deal intuitively with what happens to objects when they move at Einsteinian speeds through Einsteinian spaces, or with the sheer weirdness of objects too small to deserve the name 'object' at all. Yet somehow the emergent power of our evolved brains has enabled us to develop the crystalline edifice of mathematics by which we accurately predict the behaviour of entities that lie under the radar of our intuitive comprehension. This, too, makes me proud to be human, although to my regret I am not among the mathematically gifted of my species.

Less rarefied but still proud-making is the advanced, and continually advancing, technology that surrounds us in our everyday lives. Your smartphone, your laptop computer, the satnav in your car and the satellites that feed it, your car itself, the giant airliner that can loft not just its own weight plus passengers and cargo but also the 120 tons of fuel it ekes out over a thirteen-hour journey of seven thousand miles.

Less familiar, but destined to become more so, is 3D printing. A computer 'prints' a solid object, say a chess bishop, by depositing a sequence of layers, a process radically and interestingly different from the biological version of '3D printing' which is embryology. A 3D printer can make an exact copy of an existing object. One technique is to feed the computer a series of photographs of the object to be copied, taken from all different angles. The computer does the formidably complicated mathematics to synthesize the specification of the solid shape by integrating the angular views. There may be life forms in the universe that make their children in this body-scanning kind of way, but our own reproduction is instructively different. This, incidentally, is why almost all biology textbooks are seriously wrong when they describe DNA as a 'blueprint' for life. DNA may be a blueprint for protein, but it is not a blueprint for a baby. It's more like a recipe or a computer program.

We are not arrogant, not hubristic, to celebrate the sheer bulk and detail of what we know through science. We are simply telling the honest and irrefutable truth.

Also honest is the frank admission of how much we don't yet know – how much more work remains to be done. That is the very antithesis of hubristic arrogance. Science combines a massive contribution, in volume and detail, of what we do know with humility in proclaiming what we don't. Religion, by embarrassing contrast, has contributed literally zero to what we know, combined with huge hubristic confidence in the alleged facts it has simply made up.

But I want to suggest a further and less obvious point about the contrast of religion with atheism. I want to argue that the atheistic worldview has an unsung virtue of intellectual courage. I'll begin with what may seem like a digression.

Fred Hoyle's *The Black Cloud*,[1] one of the best science-fiction novels I have ever read (despite its obnoxious hero), does what good science fiction should: while entertaining, it informs and widens thought about real science. The black cloud is an alien creature of superhuman intelligence which parks itself in orbit around the sun in order to feed on solar energy. Scientists eventually establish communication, and much drama ensues. As the novel reaches its climax, they ask the cloud to pass on its knowledge, which is as far beyond these physicists as their knowledge is beyond that of, say, Aristotle. The cloud

---

[1] Fred Hoyle, *The Black Cloud* (London: Heinemann, 1957).

agrees but explains that the flashing-light code by which it will impart its knowledge is best aimed at only one human at a time. A brilliant young physicist called Dave Weichart volunteers for the hot seat. Eventually he falls into a trance from which he never recovers, and dies of an overheated brain. The same happens, after a longer wrestle, to Christopher Kingsley, the astrophysicist hero of the story. Human brains, even those of world-class physicists, are simply not equipped to cope with super-human knowledge.

The cloud departs for another part of the galaxy on an urgent mission. It explains that, despite its gargantuan knowledge, there are certain problems labelled as the Deep Problems, which are beyond even its understanding. Like any good scientist, the superhuman black cloud has the humility to know what it doesn't know. The reason for its departure is that a neighbouring black cloud, only a few light-years away, announced that it had found a solution to the Deep Problems (presumably something other than 42). Since that announcement, no further communication has been received, and our cloud, as its nearest neighbour, feels a duty to go and investigate whether the discoverer is dead or survives to pass on the long-sought answer to the Deep Problems. The reader is led to suspect that the neighbouring cloud died from an elevated version of the lethal overheating that killed Weichart and Kingsley.

What are the Deep Problems for us? What are the questions that might forever be beyond our reach? In the early nineteenth century, how complex life came to exist and diversify would have sprung first to mind, but those questions have now been definitively answered by Darwin and his successors. I suppose the remaining deep questions are things like: 'How does brain physiology produce subjective consciousness?' 'Where do the laws of physics come from?' 'What set the fundamental physical constants, and why do they appear fine-tuned to produce us?' and 'Why is there something rather than nothing?' The fact that science can't (yet) answer these questions testifies to science's humility. It most certainly doesn't imply that religion can. Science may or may not, during the next century or so, solve these Deep Problems. And if science – including the science of evolved superhuman aliens – can't answer them, nothing can. Certainly not theology.

But I said I was going to make a point about the intellectual courage of the atheistic worldview, and I'll do it in the context of the Deep Problems. Why is there something rather than nothing? Our physicist colleague Lawrence Krauss, in his book *A Universe from Nothing*,[1] controversially suggests that, for quantum-theoretic

---

[1] Lawrence M. Krauss, *A Universe from Nothing: Why There is Something rather than Nothing* (New York: Free Press, 2012).

reasons, Nothing (the capital letter is deliberate) is unstable. Just as matter and antimatter annihilate each other to make Nothing, so the reverse can happen. A random quantum fluctuation causes matter and antimatter to spring spontaneously out of Nothing. Krauss's critics largely focus on the definition of Nothing. His version may not be what everybody understands by nothing, but at least it is supremely simple – as simple it must be, if it is to satisfy us as the base of a 'crane' explanation (Dan Dennett's phrase), such as cosmic inflation or evolution. It is simple compared to the world that followed from it by largely understood processes: the big bang, inflation, galaxy formation, star formation, element formation in the interior of stars, supernova explosions blasting the elements into space, condensation of element-rich dust clouds into rocky planets such as Earth, the laws of chemistry by which, on this planet at least, the first self-replicating molecule arose, then evolution by natural selection and the whole of biology which is now, at least in principle, understood.

Why did I speak of intellectual courage? Because the human mind, including my own, rebels emotionally against the idea that something as complex as life, and the rest of the expanding universe, could have 'just happened'. It takes intellectual courage to kick yourself out of your emotional incredulity and persuade yourself that there is no other rational choice.

On a smaller scale, it recalls my emotional response to a really good trick by a world-class conjuror: Jamy Ian Swiss, say, or Derren Brown, or Penn and Teller. Emotion screams: 'It's a miracle! It's just got to be supernatural,' almost drowning out the still small voice of reason: 'No, it's just a trick, there really is a rational explanation.' The still small voice takes on the patient (as I imagine) Scottish tones of David Hume: 'Which is more probable, that the impossible has really happened or that the conjuror has fooled you?' You don't have to understand how the trick was done in order to take the courageous leap of reason and say: 'Hard as it is to swallow, I know it's only a trick. The laws of physics are secure.'

Move from the conjuring trick to the universe. Again, emotion screams: 'No, it's too much to believe! You are trying to tell me the entire universe, including me and the trees and the Great Barrier Reef and the Andromeda Galaxy and a tardigrade's finger, all came about by mindless atomic collisions, no supervisor, no architect? You cannot be serious. All this complexity and glory stemmed from Nothing and a random quantum fluctuation? Give me a break.' And again, reason quietly and soberly replies: 'Yes. Most of the steps in the chain are well understood, although until recently they weren't. In the case of the biological steps, they've been understood since 1859. But more important, even if we never understand all the steps, nothing can change the principle that, however improbable the entity you are trying to explain, postulating a creator god doesn't help you, because the god would itself need exactly the same kind of explanation.' However difficult it may be to explain the origin of simplicity, the spontaneous arising of complexity is, by definition, more improbable. And a creative intelligence capable of designing a universe would have to be supremely improbable and supremely in need of explanation in its own right. However improbable the naturalistic answer to the riddle of existence, the theistic alternative is even more so. But it needs a courageous leap of reason to accept the conclusion.

This is what I meant when I said the atheistic worldview requires intellectual courage. It requires moral courage, too. As an atheist, you abandon your imaginary friend, you forgo the comforting props of a celestial father figure to bail you out of trouble. You are going to die, and you'll never see your dead loved ones again. There's no holy book to tell you what to do, tell you what's right or wrong. You are an intellectual adult. You must face up to life, to moral decisions. But there is dignity in that grown-up courage. You stand tall and face into the keen wind of reality. You have company: warm, human arms around you, and a legacy of culture which has built up not only scientific knowledge and the material comforts that applied science brings but also art, music, the rule of law, and civilized discourse on morals. Morality and standards for life can be built up by intelligent design – design by real, intelligent humans who actually exist. Atheists have the intellectual courage to accept reality for what it is: wonderfully and shockingly explicable. As an atheist, you have the moral courage to live to the full the only life you're ever going to get: to fully inhabit reality, rejoice in it, and do your best finally to leave it better than you found it.

LETTING THE NEIGHBOURS KNOW
DANIEL C. DENNETT

It is easy to misjudge the effects of one's public actions. It can be tempting to overestimate their influence, taking undue credit for a trend that was already simmering. Others have highlighted our meeting as the catalyst for what might be called the Great Reaction that is emptying churches around the world, but none of us has ever endorsed that simple view, gratifying though it would be. Just as likely is the opposite misjudgement: undervaluing the supportive role that can be played by a few well-placed and well-timed declarations. Memes can go viral today at near the speed of light, thanks to the new transparency brought about by the worldwide adoption of the internet and its supporting devices (and don't forget radios and television).

MIT Media Lab professor Deb Roy and I highlighted these prospects a few years ago in a *Scientific American* article comparing today's upheaval with the hugely creative but also destructive Cambrian Explosion of 543 million years ago.[1] The Australian zoologist Andrew Parker has advanced the hypothesis that a chemical change which rendered the shallow ocean more transparent triggered that veritable Olympiad of evolutionary arms races, both extinguishing ancient branches and generating novel branches on the Tree of Life.[2] Whether or not Parker is basically right about the Cambrian Explosion – and for what it is worth, I think he is – there can be little doubt about the Internet Explosion we are experiencing today.

> We can now see further, faster, and more cheaply and easily than ever before – and we can be seen. And you and I can see that everyone can see what we see, in a recursive hall of mirrors of mutual knowledge that both enables and hobbles. The age-old game of hide-and-seek that has shaped all life on the planet has suddenly shifted its playing field, its equipment and its rules. The players who cannot adjust will not last long.[3]

[1] Daniel C. Dennett and Deb Roy, 'Our transparent future', *Scientific American*, March 2015.

[2] Andrew Parker, *In the Blink of an Eye: How Vision Sparked the Big Bang of Evolution* (New York: Basic Books, 2003).

[3] Dennett and Roy, 'Our transparent future', p. 67.

Certainly the rise of the New Atheism was enabled in large measure by this expansion of mutual knowledge. Some of your best friends may be atheists, and you may know that, but now almost everybody knows that almost everybody knows that some of almost everybody's best friends are atheists – which makes it much less daunting and dangerous to 'come out' as an atheist. There is strength in numbers, but much more strength when the numbers know roughly how numerous they are. It permits a measure of coordination, which doesn't even have to be carefully reasoned out. It has recently been shown that bacteria – which are about as uncomprehending as a living thing can be – engage in *quorum sensing*, delaying their commitment to a new simple strategy until they have detected enough allies in the neighbourhood to mount a mass action.

There is another relatively subtle effect that can be achieved by everyday folks. You don't have to be politically powerful or famous or eloquent or even notably influential in your community: you can be a *sacrificial anode*. The term sounds both dangerous and religious, but it is neither. It is well known among sailors and fishermen and others who work on boats and ships, and it goes by other names: *cathodic protection system*, or just *zinc*, or sometimes – a term I like because it conjures up such shocking images – *sacrificial plate*. (Did you just picture the head of John the Baptist on Salome's serving platter?)

DANIEL C. DENNETT

When a steel boat or ship with a bronze or brass propeller sits in salt water, a battery of sorts is created, with electrons flowing spontaneously from steel to the alloy, eating it away at an alarming rate. A brand new solid-brass propeller can become pitted in a few days and destroyed in a few months; painting it with some protective shield is ineffective. The solution: bolt a small piece of zinc (other metals will work, but zinc for various reasons is best) to the steel (alternatively, thread a zinc nut of sorts on to the stainless steel propeller shaft) and your problem is solved. The modest piece of zinc, being galvanically more active than the brass or bronze alloy, 'takes all the heat' (the current) and allows itself to be sacrificed in order to protect the part that needs to do the heavy work. Once a year, you can easily replace the almost-depleted piece of zinc with a new sacrificial anode.

The political moral to be drawn from this analogy is obvious. If you are, say, a US senator or representative, or other official whose effectiveness would be seriously diminished by a reputation for extremism (in any dimension or direction), it helps mightily to have others a little further out there, visible and undaunted, who can tolerate being seen as 'too radical' because their livelihoods and security don't depend (much) on such a reputation. Since those on either side of any political divide are motivated to caricature and exaggerate the opinions of

30

the opposition, effective political advocacy depends on being able to disavow slightly more galvanically active opinions held by some of the folks on one's own side of things.

There are limits, to be sure. As in any other arms race, there is a dynamic interplay, and if polarization becomes too extreme – with many people all too willing to be sacrificial anodes for their favourite politicians – the value of the strategic principle evaporates. But here is where the frank and open expression of one's actual views – however boring and middle-of-the-road they seem to you to be – can do some valuable work. Just calmly letting the neighbours know that you are in favour of x, disapprove of y, think z is not to be trusted – in short, being not just an informed citizen but an informing citizen – can substantially contribute to the reduction of polarization and the gradual displacement of received opinion in the directions you favour.

The diversity of opinions among the four of us provides a good example of these factors at work. For once in my life, I get to play 'good cop', because I believe that we should be concerned to preserve the good that organized religions *can* do. Does religion 'poison everything', as my dear, late friend Hitch insisted on saying?[1] Only in a very

---

[1] Christopher Hitchens, *God Is Not Great: How Religion Poisons Everything* (New York: Twelve Books, 2007).

attenuated sense, I think. Many things are quite harmless in moderation and poisonous only in quantity. I understand why Hitch emphasized this view; as a foreign correspondent he had much first-hand, dangerous experience with the worst features of religion, while I know of all that only at second hand – often from his reportage. I, in contrast, have known people whose lives would be desolate and friendless if it weren't for the non-judgemental welcome they have received in one religious organization or another. I regret the residual irrationalism valorized by almost all religion, but I don't see the state playing the succouring, comforting role well, so until we find secular successor organizations to take up that humane task, I am not in favour of ushering churches off the scene. I would rather assist in transforming these organizations into forms that are not caught in the trap of irrational – and necessarily insincere – allegiance to patent nonsense.

There are denominations that already have succeeded in this maturation, and I applaud them. Richard and Sam have their variant opinions on these matters, and we don't hesitate to express our disagreements to each other when they arise, but these are all – so far as I know – respectful and constructive differences of opinion. Any who search the transcription of our discussion for either a monolithic shared creed or a contradiction suppressed for political reasons will come up empty-handed. It is always amusing to hear us accused of having our own 'faith', our own 'religion' – as if to say: 'You atheists are just as unpresentable as we religionists are!' – when the only shared dogma they can point to is our trust in truth, evidence and honest persuasion. That is not blind faith but just the opposite: faith continually tested, corrected and provisionally defended by the testimony of our senses and our common sense. Unlike proselytizers for any religion, we gladly accept the burden of proof for the positions we defend, and we never retreat to any holy texts or *ex cathedra* pronouncements.

IN GOOD COMPANY

SAM HARRIS

Ever since the phrase 'the New Atheists' appeared in print, I have found myself celebrated or abused in the same breath with Richard Dawkins, Daniel Dennett and Christopher Hitchens. Needless to say, I've been greatly honoured by the association. It has, however, conveyed a false sense that we often schemed together in person. Although two or three of us would occasionally meet at conferences or other events, the book you are about to read provides a transcript of the only conversation the four of us ever had.

Christopher died in 2011, which gives this record a special poignancy. There is no question that his absence has been keenly felt in recent years. More times than I can count, strangers have come forward to say, 'I miss Hitch.' Their words are always uttered in protest over some fresh crime against reason or good taste. They are spoken after a bully passes by, smirking and unchallenged, whether on the left or on the right. They have become a mantra of sorts, intoned without any hope of effect, in the face of dangerous banalities or lies. Often, I hear in them a note of reproach. Sometimes it's intended.

I, too, miss Hitch. But I will resist the temptation to offer further eulogy here. After all, the time will come when the rest of us have also left the stage. However, it seems that a record of our conversation will remain. We filmed it almost as an afterthought. I'm very glad we did.

Treating Richard, Dan, Christopher and me as a four-headed atheist has always elided significant differences of emphasis and opinion, but it was fair enough on the important points: Is there a distinction between believing things for good reasons and believing them for bad ones? Do science and religion differ in the degree to which they observe this distinction? Put this way, the debate is over before it even begins.

However disparate our interests, each of us was acutely aware that religious dogmatism hinders the growth of honest knowledge and divides humanity to no necessary purpose. The latter is a dangerous irony, of course, because one of religion's most vaunted powers is that it *unites* people. It does that too, but generally by amplifying tribalism and spawning moralistic fears that would not otherwise exist. The fact that sane men and women can often be found doing good for God's sake is no rejoinder here, because faith gives them bad reasons for doing good when good reasons are available. These are points that each of the four of us has made again and again, whether to applause or to stony silence.

In truth, not much need be said to close the door on belief in an omniscient, omnipotent and benevolent deity of the sort imagined by Christians, Muslims and Jews. Open any newspaper, and what do you find?

Today, a set of identical twin girls born with microcephaly in Brazil. How does something like this happen? Their mother was bitten by a mosquito carrying the Zika virus – which God, in his abundance, also made. Among the many unhappy effects of this virus is to produce tiny heads, tiny brains, and commensurately tiny lives for the offspring of any woman unlucky enough to be infected.

Imagine the woman herself a few months ago, doing everything within her power to prepare a happy life for her unborn daughters. Where does she work? A factory. How often does she pray? Daily, no doubt.

But at the crucial moment she sleeps. Perhaps she's dreaming of a world better than the one we live in. Picture a lone mosquito finding her open window. Picture it alighting upon her exposed arm. Will an omnipotent, omniscient and wholly benevolent God muster the slightest defence? Not even a breeze. The mosquito's proboscis pierces her skin immediately. What are the faithful to believe at this point? One suspects they know that their

God isn't nearly as attentive as he would be if he actually existed.

So there was nothing to stop this tiny monster – descended from a long line of monsters that have been spreading disease for some 200 million years – from drinking this woman's innocent blood and, in return for a meal, destroying the lives of her unborn girls.

The facts of a single case dismantle whole libraries of theological hairsplitting and casuistry. And yet the horror compounds. Picture the woman noticing the welt on her arm the next morning – just a minor annoyance in a life soon to be filled with tragedy. Perhaps she's heard reports of Zika and knows how the virus is spread. Her prayers now acquire a special fervour. To what end? Can the consolations of a faith so utterly misplaced outweigh the irony of worshipping a deity this impotent or evil – or, indeed, imaginary?

In the absence of God, we find true sources of hope and consolation. Art, literature, sport, philosophy – along with other forms of creativity and contemplation – do not require ignorance or lies to be enjoyed. And then there is science – which, apart from its intrinsic rewards, will be the true source of mercy in the present case. When a vaccine or a cure for Zika is finally found, preventing untold misery and death, will the faithful thank God for it?

No doubt they will. And so these conversations must continue . . .

THE FOUR HORSEMEN:
A DISCUSSION

RICHARD DAWKINS, DANIEL C. DENNETT,
SAM HARRIS, CHRISTOPHER HITCHENS

WASHINGTON DC — 30 SEPTEMBER 2007

PART I

RICHARD DAWKINS: One of the things we've all met is the accusation that we are strident or arrogant or vitriolic or shrill. What do we think about that?

DANIEL C. DENNETT: Yes. Well, I'm amused by it because I went out of my way in my book to address reasonable religious people,[1] and I test-flew the draft with groups of students who were deeply religious. And indeed, the first draft incurred some real anguish. So I made adjustments and made adjustments, and it didn't do any good in the end, because I still got hammered for being rude and aggressive. And I came to realize that it's a no-win situation. It's a mug's game. The religions have contrived to make it impossible to disagree with them critically without being rude.

[1] Daniel C. Dennett, *Breaking the Spell: Religion as a Natural Phenomenon* (New York: Viking Adult, 2006).

DAWKINS: Without being rude.

DENNETT: You know, they sort of play the hurt-feelings card at every opportunity, and you're faced with the choice of, Well, am I going to be rude? Or am I going to—

DAWKINS: Say nothing, yes.

DENNETT: —articulate this criticism? Or I mean am I going to articulate it or am I just going to button my lip and—?

SAM HARRIS: Well, that's what it is to trespass a taboo. I think we're all encountering the fact that religion is held off the table of rational criticism in some kind of formal way, even by, we're discovering, our fellow secularists and our fellow atheists. It leaves people to their own superstitions. Even if it's abject and causing harm, don't look too closely at it.

DENNETT: That was of course the point of the title of my book; there is this spell, and we've got to break it.

CHRISTOPHER HITCHENS: But if the charge of offensiveness in general is to be allowed in public discourse, then without self-pity I think we should say that we too can be offended and insulted. I mean, I'm not just in disagreement when someone like Tariq Ramadan,[1]

---

[1] Tariq Ramadan (b. 1962): Swiss Islamic academic and writer; Professor of Contemporary Islamic Studies at Oxford University.

accepted at the high tables of Oxford University as a spokesman, says the most he'll demand when it comes to the stoning of women is a moratorium on it. I find that profoundly much more than annoying. Not only insulting but actually threatening.

HARRIS: But you're not offended. I don't see you taking things personally. You're alarmed by the liabilities of certain ways of thinking, as in Ramadan's case.

HITCHENS: Yes, but he would say, or people like him would say, that if I doubt the historicity of the prophet Mohammed, I've injured them in their deepest feelings. Well, I am, in fact – and I think all people ought to be – offended, at least in their deepest integrity, by, say, the religious proposition that without a supernatural, celestial dictatorship we wouldn't know right from wrong.

HARRIS: But are you really offended by that? Doesn't it just seem wrong to you?

HITCHENS: No, I say only, Sam, that if the offensiveness charge is to be allowed in general, and arbitrated by the media, then I think we're entitled to claim that much, without being self-pitying or representing ourselves as an oppressed minority. Which I think is an opposite danger, I would admit. Mind you, I also agree with Daniel that there's no way in which the charge against us can be completely avoided, because what we say does offend the core, the very core, of any serious religious person, in the same way. We deny the divinity of Jesus, for example. Many people will be terrifically shocked and possibly hurt. It's just too bad.

DAWKINS: I'm fascinated by the contrast between the amount of offence that's taken by religion and the amount of offence that people take against nearly anything else. Like artistic taste. Your taste in music, your taste in art, your politics. You can be, not exactly as rude as you like, but you can be far, far more rude about such things. And I'd quite like to try to quantify that, to actually do research about it. To test people with statements about their favourite football team, or their favourite piece of music, or something, and see how far you can go before they take offence. Is there anything else, apart from, say, how ugly your face is [*laughter*], that would give such—?

HITCHENS: Or your husband's or wife's or girlfriend's faces. Well, it's interesting that you say that, because I regularly debate with a terrible man called Bill Donohue of the Catholic League,[1] and he actually is righteously upset by certain trends in modern art, which tend to draw attention to themselves by blasphemy.

HARRIS: *Piss Christ.*

---

[1] Bill Donohue (b. 1947): US sociologist; President of the Catholic League for Religious and Civil Rights.

HITCHENS: Yes, for example, Serrano's *Piss Christ*,[1] or the elephant dung on the Virgin.[2] And indeed, I think it's quite important that we share with Sophocles and other pre-monotheists a revulsion to desecration or to profanity. That we don't want to see churches desecrated.

DAWKINS: No, indeed not.

HITCHENS: Religious icons trashed, and so forth. We share an admiration for at least some of the aesthetic achievements of religion.

HARRIS: I think our criticism is actually more barbed than that. We're not merely offending people, we're also telling them that they're wrong to be offended.

ALL: Yes.

HARRIS: Physicists aren't offended when their view of physics is disproved or challenged. This is just not the way rational minds operate when they're really trying to get at what's true in the world. Religions purport to be representing reality, and yet there's this peevish, and tribal, and ultimately dangerous response to having these ideas challenged.

DENNETT: Well, and too, there's no polite way to say to somebody—

[1] Andres Serrano (b. 1950): US artist and photographer.

[2] *The Holy Virgin Mary* (1996) by British artist Christopher Ofili (b. 1968).

HARRIS: 'You've wasted your life!'

DENNETT: '—Do you realize you've wasted your life? Do you realize you've just devoted all your efforts and all your goods to the glorification of something that's just a myth?' Even if you say, 'Have you even considered the possibility that maybe you've wasted your life on this?' There's no inoffensive way of saying that. But we do have to say it, because they should jolly well consider it. Same as we do about our own lives.

DAWKINS: Dan Barker's[1] making a collection of clergymen who've lost their faith but don't dare say so, because it's their only living. It's the only thing they know how to do.

HARRIS: Yes, I've heard from one of them, at least.

DAWKINS: Have you?

HITCHENS: I used to run into this when I was younger, in arguments with members of the Communist Party. They sort of knew that it was all up with the Soviet Union. Many of them had suffered a lot and sacrificed a great deal and struggled manfully to keep what they thought was the great ideal alive. Their mainspring had broken, but they couldn't give it up because it would involve a similar concession. But certainly, if

---

[1] Daniel Barker (b. 1949): US atheist activist and former Christian preacher; joint President of the Freedom from Religion Foundation. Dan Barker's collection was one of the strands later woven into 'The Clergy Project': see https://en.wikipedia.org/wiki/The_Clergy_Project.

anyone had said to me, 'How could you say that to them about the Soviet Union? Didn't you know you were going to really make them cry and hurt their feelings?' I would have said, 'Don't be ridiculous. Don't be absurd.' But I find it in many cases almost an exactly analogous argument.

DENNETT: When people tell me I'm being rude and vicious and terribly aggressive in a way, I say, 'If I were saying these things about the pharmaceutical industry or the oil interests, would it be rude? Would it be off limits? No.'

DAWKINS: Of course it wouldn't.

DENNETT: Well, I want religion to be treated just the way we treat the pharmaceuticals and the oil industry. I'm not against pharmaceutical companies – I'm against some of the things they do – but I just want to put religions on the same page with them.

HITCHENS: Including denying them tax exemptions, or, in the English case, state subsidies.

DENNETT: Yes.

DAWKINS: I'm curious how religion acquired this charmed status that it has, compared to other things. Somehow we've all bought into it, whether we're religious or not. And some historical process has led to this immunization of religion, this hyper-offence-taking that religion is allowed to take.

DENNETT: What's particularly amusing to me, finally – and at first it infuriated me, but now I'm amused – is that they've managed to enlist legions of non-religious people who take offence on their behalf.

DAWKINS: And how!

DENNETT: In fact, the most vicious reviews of my book have been by people who are not themselves religious but they're terribly afraid of hurting the feelings of the people who are religious, and they chastise me worse than anybody who's actually religious.

DAWKINS: Exactly my experience.

HARRIS: And I think one of you pointed out how condescending that view is. It's like the idea of penitentiaries: Other people need them; we must keep the felons safely confined.

There's one answer to that question which may illuminate a difference I have with, I think, all three of you. I still use words like 'spiritual' and 'mystical' without furrowing my brow too much, to the consternation of many atheists. I think there is a range of experience that's rare and is only talked about – without obvious qualms – in religious discourse. And because it's only talked about in religious discourse, it is just riddled with superstition, and it's used to justify various metaphysical schemes – which it can't reasonably do. But clearly people do have extraordinary experiences, whether they have them on LSD or they have them because they sat alone in a cave for a year, or because they just happen to have a nervous system that's especially labile. People can have self-transcending experiences, and religion seems to be the only game in town when talking about those experiences and dignifying them. So this is one reason it's taboo to criticize it, because we're talking about the most important moments in people's lives and we appear to be trashing them, at least from their point of view.

DAWKINS: Well, I don't have to agree with you, Sam, in order to say that it's very good that you're saying that sort of thing. Because it shows that, as you say, religion is not the only game in town when it comes to being spiritual. Just as it's a good idea to have somebody from the political right who's an atheist, because otherwise there's a confusion of values, which doesn't help us, and it's much better to have this diversity in other areas. But I think I sort of do agree with you, but even if I didn't, I'd think it was valuable to have that.

HITCHENS: If we could make one change, and only one, mine would be to distinguish the numinous from the supernatural. You, Sam, had a marvellous quotation in your blog from Francis Collins,[1] the genome pioneer, who said whilst mountaineering one day he was just overcome by the landscape and then went down

---

[1] Francis Collins (b. 1950): US geneticist and physician; Director of the National Institutes of Health, Bethesda, Md.

on his knees and accepted Jesus Christ.[1] A complete non-sequitur.

HARRIS: Exactly.

HITCHENS: It's never even been suggested that Jesus Christ created that landscape.

HARRIS: A frozen waterfall in three streams put him in mind of the Trinity.

HITCHENS: Absolutely! We're all triune in one way or another. We're programmed for that. That's very clear. It wouldn't ever have been a four-headed God. [*Laughter*] You know that from experience.

But that would be an enormous distinction to make, and I think it would clear up a lot of people's confusion – that what we have in our emotions, the surplus value of our personalities, aren't particularly useful for our evolution. Or we can't prove they are. But they do belong to us, all the same. They don't belong to the supernatural and are not to be conscripted or annexed by any priesthood.

DENNETT: It's a sad fact that people won't, in a sense, trust their own valuing of their numinous experiences. They think it isn't really as good as it seems unless it's from God, unless it's some kind of a proof of religion. No, it's just as wonderful as it seems. It's just as

---

[1] https://www.samharris.org/blog/item/the-strange-case-of-francis-collins.

important. It is the best moment in your life, and it's the moment when you forget yourself and become better than you ever thought you could be, in some way, and you see, in all humbleness, the wonderfulness of nature. That's it! And that's wonderful. But it doesn't add anything to say, 'Golly, that has to have been given to me by Somebody even more wonderful.'

DAWKINS: It's been hijacked, hasn't it?

HITCHENS: It's also, I think, a deformity or shortcoming in the human personality, frankly. Because religion keeps stressing how humble it is, and how meek it is, and how accepting, almost to the point of self-abnegation it is. But actually it makes extraordinarily arrogant claims for these moments. It says, 'I suddenly realized that the universe was all about *me*. And felt terrifically humble about it.' Come on! We can laugh people out of that, I believe. And I think we must.

DENNETT: And I am so tired of 'If only Professor Dennett had the humility to *blah, blah, blah.*' And humility, humility. [*Laughter*] And this, from people of breathtaking arrogance.

HITCHENS: They shove one aside saying, 'Don't mind me, I'm on an errand for God.' How modest is that?

HARRIS: This is a point I think we should return to: this notion of the arrogance of science. Because there is no discourse that enforces humility more rigorously than

51

science. Scientists in my experience are the first people to say they don't know. If you get scientists to start talking outside their area of specialization, they immediately start hedging their bets, saying things like, 'I'm sure there's someone in the room who knows more about this than I do, and, of course, all the data aren't in.' This is the mode of discourse in which we're most candid about the scope of our ignorance.

HITCHENS: Well, actually, a lot of academics come out with that kind of false modesty. But I do know what you mean.

DAWKINS: Any academic should do that. The thing about religious people is that they recite the Nicene Creed every week, which says precisely what they believe. There are three Gods, not one. The Virgin Mary, Jesus died, went to the . . . what was it? Down for three days and then came up again – in precise detail, and yet they have the gall to accuse us of being overconfident, and of not knowing what it is to doubt.

DENNETT: I don't think many of them ever let themselves contemplate the question which I think scientists ask themselves all the time: 'What if I'm wrong?' 'What if I'm wrong?' It's just not part of their repertory.

HITCHENS: Would you mind if I disagree with you about that?

DENNETT: No.

HITCHENS: A lot of the talk that makes religious people not hard to beat, but hard to argue with, is precisely that they'll say they're in a permanent crisis of faith. There is, indeed, a prayer: 'Lord, I believe. Help thou my unbelief.' Graham Greene says the great thing about being a Catholic was that it was a challenge to his unbelief.[1] A lot of people live by keeping two sets of books.

DENNETT: Yes.

DAWKINS: Exactly.

HITCHENS: It's my impression that a majority of the people I know who call themselves believers, or people of faith, do that all the time. I wouldn't say it was schizophrenia; that *would* be rude. But they're quite aware of the implausibility of what they say. They don't act on it when they go to the doctor, or when they travel, or anything of this kind. But in some sense they couldn't be without it. But they're quite respectful of the idea of doubt. In fact, they try and build it in when they can.

DAWKINS: Well, that's interesting then. So when they're reciting the creed with its total sort of apparent conviction, this is a kind of mantra which is forcing them to

---

[1] Graham Greene (1904–91): English novelist; converted to Catholicism just before his marriage; later described himself as a 'Catholic atheist'.

overcome doubt by saying, 'Yes, I do believe, I do believe, I do believe!' Because really they don't.

DENNETT: Sure. And—

HITCHENS: And of course, like their secular counterparts, they're glad other people believe it. It's an affirmation they wouldn't want other people not to be making.

DAWKINS: Yes, yes.

HARRIS: Well, also there's this curious bootstrapping move, where they start with the premise that belief without evidence is especially noble. This is the doctrine of faith. This is the parable of Doubting Thomas. So they start with that and then add this notion, which has been hurled at me in various debates, that the fact that people can believe without evidence is itself a subtle form of evidence. Francis Collins, whom you mentioned, brings this up in his book.[1] The fact that we have this intuition of God is itself some subtle form of evidence. And it's a kind of kindling phenomenon: once you say it's good to start without evidence, the fact that you can proceed is a subtle form of evidence, and then the demand for any more evidence is itself a kind of corruption of the intellect, or a temptation, to be guarded against, and you get a kind of perpetual-motion machine of self-deception, once you can get this thing up and running.

[1] Francis Collins, *The Language of God* (New York: Free Press, 2006).

HITCHENS: But they like the idea that it can't be demonstrated, because then there'd be nothing to be faithful about. If everyone had seen the Resurrection and we all knew that we'd been saved by it, well, then we would be living in an unalterable system of belief, and it would have to be policed. Those of us who don't believe in it are very glad it's not true, because we think it would be horrible. Those who do believe it don't want it to be absolutely proven so there can't be any doubt about it, because then there's no wrestling with conscience, there are no dark nights of the soul.

HARRIS: There was a review of one of our books, I don't remember which, but it made exactly that point: what a crass expectation on the part of atheists that there should be total evidence for any of this. There would be much less magic if everyone was compelled to believe by too much evidence. Actually, this was Francis Collins.

HITCHENS: Well, a friend of mine – Canon Fenton of Oxford,[1] actually – said that if the Church validated the Holy Shroud of Turin, he personally would leave the ranks. [*Laughter*] Because if they were doing things like that, he didn't want any part of it. I didn't expect, when I started off my book tour, to be as lucky

---

[1] John Fenton (1921–2008): Anglican priest and theologian; Canon of Christ Church, Oxford, 1978–91.

as I was; Jerry Falwell[1] died on my first week on the road. That was amazing. And I didn't expect Mother Teresa[2] to come out as an atheist. [*Laughter*] But reading her letters, which I now have, it's rather interesting. She writes that she can't bring herself to believe any of this. She tells all her confessors, all her superiors, that she can't hear a voice, can't feel a presence, even in the Mass, even in the sacraments. No small thing. They write back to her, saying, 'That's good, that's great, you're suffering, it gives you a share in the Crucifixion, it makes you part of Calvary.' You can't beat an argument like that. The less you believe it, the more it's a demonstration of faith.

HARRIS: The more you prove it's true.

HITCHENS: Yes, and the struggle, the dark night of the soul, is the proof in itself. So, we just have to realize that these really are non-overlapping magisteria. We can't hope to argue with a mentality of this kind.

DENNETT: We can do just what you're doing now. That is, we can say, 'Look at this interesting bag of tricks that have evolved. Notice that they are circular, that they're self-sustaining, that they could be about

---

[1] Jerry Falwell (1933–2007): US Southern Baptist pastor and evangelist; co-founder in 1979 of the Moral Majority.

[2] Agnes Gonxha Bojaxhiu (1910–97), known as Mother Teresa: Catholic nun and missionary; founder in 1950 of the order of the 'Missionaries of Charity'.

anything.' And then you don't argue with them, you simply point out that these are not valid ways of thinking about *anything*. Because you could use the very same tricks to sustain something which was manifestly fraudulent.

And in fact, what fascinates me is that a lot of the tricks have their counterparts with con artists, who use the very same forms of non-argument, the very same non sequiturs, and they make, for instance, a virtue out of trust. And as soon as you start exhibiting any suspicion of the con man, he gets all hurt on you and plays the hurt-feelings card, and reminds you how wonderful taking it on faith is. There aren't any new tricks; these tricks have evolved over countless years.

HITCHENS: And one could add the production of bogus special effects as well. One of the things that completely convicts religion of being fraudulent is the belief in the miraculous. The same people will say, 'Well, Einstein felt a spiritual force in the universe,' when what he said was the whole point about it is that there are no miracles. There are no changes in the natural order, that's the miraculous thing. They're completely cynical about claiming him.

HARRIS: And every religious person makes the same criticism of other religions that we do. They reject the pseudo-miracles and the pseudo-claims and certainties of others. They see the confidence tricks in other people's faith. And they see them rather readily. Every Christian knows that the Qur'an can't be the perfect word of the creator of the universe and that anyone who thinks it is hasn't read it closely enough. We make a very strong case when we point that out, and point out also that whatever people are experiencing in church or in prayer, no matter how positive, the fact that Buddhists and Hindus and Muslims and Christians are *all* experiencing it proves that it can't be a matter of the divinity of Jesus or the unique sanctity of the Qur'an.

DENNETT: Because there are seventeen different ways of getting there.

HITCHENS: By the way, on that tiny point, and I hope this is not a digression, it's useful to bear in mind that when you get, as I did this morning on ABC News, the question, 'Well, wouldn't you say religion did some good in the world, and there are good [religious] people?' – and you never don't get that argument, and by the way there's no reason you shouldn't – you say, 'Well, yes, I have indeed heard it said that Hamas provides social services in Gaza.' [*Laughter*] And I've even heard it said that Louis Farrakhan's group gets young black men in prison off drugs.[1] I don't know if

---

[1] Louis Walcott, later Farrakhan (b. 1933): US black nationalist and leader of the US religious group Nation of Islam.

it's true – I'm willing to accept it might be. It doesn't alter the fact that the one is a militarized terrorist organization with a fanatical anti-Semitic ideology and the second is a racist, crackpot cult. I have no doubt that Scientology gets people off drugs, too. But my insistence, always, with these people is that if you will claim it for one, you must accept it for them all. Because if you don't, it's flat-out dishonest.

HARRIS: Or you can *invent* an ideology, which, by your mere invention in that moment is obviously untrue, and which would be quite useful if propagated to billions.

HITCHENS: That's right.

HARRIS: You could say, 'Here is my new religion. Demand that your children study science and math and economics and all of our terrestrial disciplines to the best of their abilities, and if they don't persist in those efforts, they'll be tortured after death by seventeen demons.' [*Laughter*] This would be extremely useful, far more useful than Islam. And yet what are the chances that these seventeen demons exist? Zero.

DAWKINS: There's a slipperiness, too, isn't there, about one way of speaking to sophisticated intellectuals and theologians and another way of speaking to congregations and, above all, children. And I think we've all of us been accused of going after the easy targets, the

Jerry Falwells of this world, and ignoring the sophisticated professors of theology. I don't know what you feel about that, but one of the things I feel is that the sophisticated professors of theology will say one thing to each other and to intellectuals generally, but will say something totally different to a congregation. They'll talk about miracles, they'll talk about—

DENNETT: Well, they won't talk to a congregation.

DAWKINS: Well, archbishops will.

DENNETT: Yes, but when the sophisticated theologians try to talk to the preachers, the preachers won't have any of it. [*Laughs*]

DAWKINS: Well, that's true of course, yes.

DENNETT: You've got to realize that sophisticated theology is like stamp collecting. It's a very specialized thing, and only a few people do it.

DAWKINS: And of negligible influence.

DENNETT: They take in their own laundry, and they get all excited about some very arcane details, and their own religions pay almost no attention to what they're saying. A little bit of it does, of course, filter in. But it always gets beefed up again for general consumption, because what they say in their writings, at least from my experience, is eye-glazing, mind-twisting, very subtle things that have no particular bearing on life.

HITCHENS: Oh, no, I must insist! [*Laughter*] I must say a good word here for Professor Alister McGrath,[1] who in his attack on Richard said it wasn't true, as we've always been told and most Christians believe, that Tertullian said, 'Credo quia absurdum' – 'I believe it because it's ridiculous.' No, it turns out – and I've checked this now, although I don't know this from McGrath – that in fact Tertullian said the *impossibility* of it is what makes it believable.[2] That's a fine distinction, I think. [*Laughter*] And very useful for training one's mind in the finer points. In other words, the likelihood that something could have been made up is diminished by the incredibility of it. Who would try and invent something that was that unbelievable?

That actually is, I think, a debate perfectly well worth having. What I say to these people is this: You're sending your e-mail, or your letter, to the wrong address. Everyone says, 'Let's not judge religion by its fundamentalists.' All right. Take the Church of England, two of whose senior leaders recently said that the floods in North Yorkshire were the result of, among other things, homosexual behaviour – not in North Yorkshire, presumably.[3] Probably in London, I'm thinking. [*Laughter*]

[1] Alister McGrath (b. 1953): Northern Irish priest and theologian; Andreas Idreos Professor of Science and Religion at Oxford University.

[2] 'Certum est, quia impossibile': *De Carne Christi*, 5.

[3] See https://www.telegraph.co.uk/news/uknews/1556131/Floods-are-judgment-on-society-say-bishops.html, in which the Rt Rev. Graham Dow (b. 1942), Bishop of Carlisle 2000–9, is quoted to this effect.

DENNETT: God's aim is a little off. [*Laughter*]

HITCHENS: One of these, the Bishop of Liverpool,[1] was apparently in line to be the next Archbishop of Canterbury. Now, this is extraordinary. This is supposed to be the mild and reflective and thoughtful and rather troubled Church, making fanatical pronouncements. Well, I want to hear what Alister McGrath is going to write to these bishops. Is he going to say, 'Do you not realize what complete idiots you're making of yourselves and of our Church?' Did he do that? If he did it in private, I'm not impressed. He has to say it in public. Why are they telling me that I [can't] judge the Church by the statements of its bishops? I think I'm allowed to.

DAWKINS: The academic theologians, bishops and vicars will attack us for taking scriptures – or for accusing people of taking scriptures – literally: 'Of course we don't believe the Book of Genesis literally!' And yet they do preach about what Adam and Eve did, as though Adam and Eve did exist – as though they somehow have a licence to talk about things which they know, and anybody of any sophistication knows, are fictions. And yet they will talk to their congregations, their sheep, about Adam and Eve as though they did exist, as though they were factual. And a huge number of people in those congregations actually think they did exist.

[1] James Jones (b. 1948): Anglican priest; Bishop of Liverpool 1998–2013.

62

DENNETT: Can you imagine any one of these preachers saying, as such a topic is introduced, 'This is a sort of theoretical fiction. It's not true, but it's a very fine metaphor'? No. [*Laughs*]

DAWKINS: They kind of, after the fact, imply that that's what they expect you to know.

DENNETT: Yes, but they would never announce it.

HARRIS: Another point there is that they never admit how they have come to stop taking it literally. You have all these people criticizing us for our crass literalism – we're as fundamentalist as the fundamentalists – and yet these moderates don't admit how they have come to be moderate. What does moderation consist of? It consists of having *lost faith* in all of these propositions, or half of them, because of the hammer blows of science and secular politics.

DENNETT: And the crass literalism of the critics.

HARRIS: Religion has lost its mandate on a thousand questions, and moderates argue that this is somehow a triumph of faith – that faith is somehow self-enlightening. Whereas it's been enlightened from the *outside*; it's been intruded upon by science.

HITCHENS: On that point, which I was wanting to raise myself, about our own so-called fundamentalism, there's a cleric in Southwark, the first person I saw attacking you [Richard] and me in print as being just as fundamentalist as those who blew up the London Underground. Do you remember his name?

DAWKINS: I don't remember his name.

HITCHENS: He's a very senior Anglican cleric in the Diocese of Southwark.[1] I went on the BBC with him. I asked him, 'How can you call your congregation a flock? Doesn't that say everything about your religion? That you think they're sheep?' He said, 'Well, actually I used to be the pastor in New Guinea, where there aren't any sheep.' Of course, there are a lot of places where there are no sheep – the Gospel's quite hard to teach as a result. [*Laughter*] He said, 'We found out what the most important animal to the locals was, and I remember very well my local bishop rising to ask the Divine One to "Behold these swine".' [*Laughter*] His new congregation.

But this is a man who deliberately does a thing like that. That's as cynical as you could wish, and as adaptive as the day is long. And *he* says that we who doubt it are as fundamentalist as people who blow up their fellow citizens on the London Underground. It's unconscionable. Thus, I don't really mind being accused of ridiculing or treating with contempt people like that. I just, frankly, have no choice. I have the

---

[1] Colin Slee (1945–2010): Anglican cleric; Provost of Southwark from 1994; Dean from 2000 to his death.

faculty of humour, and some of it has an edge to it. I'm not going to repress that for the sake of politeness.

DENNETT: Would you think it would be good to make a distinction between the professionals and the amateurs? I share your impatience with the officials of the churches – the people who have this as their professional life. It seems to me that they know better. The congregations don't know better, because it's maintained that they should not know better. I do get very anxious about ridiculing the belief of the flock, because of the way in which they have ceded to their leaders, they've delegated authority to their leaders, and they presume their leaders are going to do it right. Who stands up and says, 'The buck stops here'? Well, it seems to me it's the preachers themselves, it's the priests, it's the bishops. And we really *should* hold their feet to the fire.

For instance, just take the issue of creationism. If somebody in a fundamentalist church thinks that creationism makes sense because their pastor told them so, well, I can understand that and excuse that. We all get a lot of what we take to be true from people whom we respect and whom we view as authorities. We don't check everything out. But where did the pastor get this idea? And I don't care where he got it. He or she is responsible because their job is to know what they're talking about, in a way that the congregation is not.

DAWKINS: We have to be a little bit careful not to sound condescending when we say that. In a way, it's reflecting the condescension of the preacher himself.

HITCHENS: Yes. Because I'll take things that you and Richard say on human natural sciences – not without wanting to check, but I'm often unable to – but knowing that you are the sort of gentlemen who would have checked. But if you say, 'The bishop told me it so I believe it,' you make a fool of yourself, it seems to me – and one is entitled to say so. Just as one is entitled, when dealing with an ordinary racist, to say that his opinions are revolting. He may know no better, but that's not going to save him from my condemnation. And nor should it. And exactly, I think it's condescending *not* to confront people, as it were, one by one or *en masse*. Public opinion is often wrong. Mob opinion is almost always wrong. Religious opinion is wrong by definition. We can't avoid this—

I wanted to introduce the name 'H. L. Mencken'[1] at this point, now a very and justly celebrated American writer. Not particularly to my taste – much too much of a Nietzschean and what really was once meant by 'social Darwinist' at one stage. But why did he win the tremendous respect of so many people in this country in the 1920s and '30s? Because he said that

[1] Henry Louis Mencken (1880–1956): US writer and scholar of American English.

the people who believe what the Methodists tell them, and what William Jennings Bryan[1] tells them, are fools. They're not *being* fooled; they *are* fools. They should—

DENNETT: Shame on them for believing this.

HITCHENS: Yes, they make themselves undignified and ignorant. No mincing of words there, and a great admixture of wit and evidence and reasoning. It absolutely works. The most successful anti-religious polemic there's probably ever been in the modern world – in the twentieth century, anyway.

HARRIS: I think we just touched upon an issue that we should highlight: this whole notion of authority. Because religious people often argue that science is just a series of uncashed cheques and we're all relying on authority: 'How do you know that the cosmological constant is . . . ?' whatever it is. So, differentiate between the kind of faith-placing in authority that we practise without fear in science, and in rationality generally, and the kind of faith-placing in the preacher or the theologian, which we criticize.

DAWKINS: But what we actually do when we, who are not physicists, take on trust what physicists say, is that we have some evidence that suggests that physicists have

---

[1] William Jennings Bryan (1860–1925): US Democratic politician and orator; anti-evolution activist, representing the World Christian Fundamentals Association at the Scopes trial of 1925.

looked into the matter – that they've done experiments, that they've peer-reviewed their papers, that they've criticized each other, that they've been subjected to massive criticism from their peers in seminars and in lectures.

DENNETT: And remember the structure that's there, too; it's not just that there's peer review. But it's very important that [science is] competitive. For instance, when Fermat's last theorem was proved by—

DAWKINS: Andrew Wiles.

DENNETT: —Andrew Wiles, the reason that those of us who said, 'Forget it, I'm never going to understand that proof,' the reason that we can be confident that it really is a proof is that—

HARRIS: Nobody wanted him to get there first. [*Laughter*]

DENNETT: —every other mathematician who was competent in the world was very well motivated to study that proof.

DAWKINS: To find it, yes.

DENNETT: And believe me, if they grudgingly admit that this is a proof, it's a proof. And there's nothing like that in religion – nothing like that!

HITCHENS: No religious person has ever been able to say what Einstein said – that if he was right, the following phenomenon would occur off the west coast of Africa during a solar eclipse. And it did, within a very tiny degree of variation. There's never been a prophecy that's been vindicated like that. Or anyone willing to place their reputation and, as it were, their life on the idea that it would be.

DAWKINS: I was once asked at a public meeting, 'Don't you think that the mysteriousness of quantum theory is just the same as the mysteriousness of the Trinity or transubstantiation?' And the answer of course is, [it] can be answered, in two quotes from Richard Feynman. One, Richard Feynman said, 'If you think you understand quantum theory, you don't understand quantum theory.' He was admitting that it's highly mysterious. The other thing is that the predictions in quantum theory experimentally are verified to the equivalent of predicting the width of North America to the width of one human hair. And so, quantum theory is massively supported by accurate predictions, even if you don't understand the mystery of the Copenhagen interpretation, whatever it is. Whereas the mystery of the Trinity doesn't even try to make a prediction, let alone an accurate one.

HITCHENS: It isn't a mystery, either.

DENNETT: I don't like the use of the word 'mystery' here. I think there's been a lot of consciousness-raising in philosophy about this term, where we have the so-called new mysterians. These are people who like the term 'mystery'. Noam Chomsky[1] is quoted as saying there are two kinds of questions – problems and mysteries. Problems are solvable, mysteries aren't.[2] First of all, I just don't buy that. But I buy the distinction, and say there's nothing about mystery in science. There are problems; there are deep problems. There are things we don't know; there are things we'll never know. But they aren't systematically incomprehensible to human beings. The glorification of the idea that these things are systematically incomprehensible I think has no place in science.

HITCHENS: Which is why I think we should be quite happy to revive traditional terms in our discourse, such as 'obscurantism' and 'obfuscation', which is what they really are. And to point out that these things can make intelligent people act stupidly. John Cornwell,[3] who's just written another attack on yourself, Richard, actually, and who is an old friend of mine, a very brilliant guy, wrote one of the best studies of the Catholic Church and fascism that has been published. In his review of you, he says that Professor Dawkins should just look at the shelves of books there are on the

---

[1] Noam Chomsky (b. 1928): US linguist and multidisciplinary scholar; highly influential in study of mind and language.

[2] Steven Pinker, *How the Mind Works* (New York: W. W. Norton, 1997), p. ix.

[3] John Cornwell (b. 1940): British academic and writer; works include *Hitler's Pope* (1999), a critical work on Pope Pius XII.

Trinity, the libraries full of attempts to solve this problem, before he's certain. But none of the books in those
religious libraries solve it either. The whole point is
that it remains insoluble, and is used to keep people
feeling baffled and inferior.

DAWKINS: I want to come back to the thing about mystery in physics. Because isn't it possible that with our
evolved brains – because we evolved in what I call Middle World, where we never have to cope with either the
very small or the cosmologically very large – we may
never actually have an intuitive feel for what's going on
in quantum mechanics. But we can still test its predictions. We can still actually do the mathematics and do
the physics to actually test the predictions – because
anybody can read the dials on an instrument.

DENNETT: Right. I think what we can see is that what
scientists have constructed, over the centuries, is a series of tools – mind tools, thinking tools, mathematical
tools and so forth – that enable us to some degree to
overcome the limitations of our evolved brains. Our
Stone Age, if you like, brains. And overcoming those
limitations is not always direct. Sometimes you have to
give up something. Yes, you'll just never be able, as you
say, to think intuitively about this. But you can know
that even though you can't think intuitively about it,
there's this laborious process by which you can make
progress. And you do have to cede a certain authority

to the process, but you can test that. And it can carry you from A to B in the same way that if you're a quadriplegic an artificial device can carry you from A to B. It doesn't mean you can walk from A to B, but you can get from A to B.

DAWKINS: That's right. And the bolder physicists will say, 'Well, who cares about intuition? I mean, just look at the maths.'

DENNETT: Yes, yes, that's right. They are comfortable with living with their prostheses.

HARRIS: Well, the perfect example of that is dimensions beyond three, because we can't visualize the fourth dimension or the fifth. But it's trivial to represent them mathematically.

DENNETT: And now we teach our undergraduates how to manipulate n-dimensional spaces, and to think about vectors in n-dimensional spaces. And they get used to the fact that they can't quite imagine them. What you do is, you imagine three of them and wave your hand a little bit, and say, 'More of the same.' But you check your intuition by running the math, and it works.

DAWKINS: Say you're a psychologist looking at personality, and you say there are fifteen dimensions of personality, and you could think of them as being fifteen dimensions in space. And anybody can see that you can imagine moving along any one of those dimensions with respect to the others, and you don't actually have to visualize fifteen-dimensional space.

DENNETT: No, and you give up that demand. And you realize, 'I can live without that. It would be nice if I could do that, but, hey, I can't see bacteria with the naked eye, either. I can live without that.'

HITCHENS: I was challenged on the radio the other day by someone who said that I believed in atoms on no evidence, because I'd never seen one. Not since George Galloway said to me that he'd never seen a barrel of oil . . .[1] [*Laughter*] But you realize that people, at this point, are wearing themselves right down to their uppers. I mean, they're desperate when they say—

I don't want us to make our lives easier, but it makes the argument a little simpler: we are quite willing to say there are many things we don't know. But what Haldane,[2] I think it was, said is that the universe is not just queerer than we suppose, it's queerer than we *can* suppose. We know there'll be great new discoveries. We know we'll live to see great things. But we know

[1] In May 2005, British anti-war activist and MP George Galloway (who would debate with Christopher Hitchens in September on the Iraq War) was alleged to have profited from the UN's oil-for-food programme in Iraq, which he denied in testimony before a US Senate committee, saying: 'I am not now, nor have I ever been, an oil trader – and neither has anyone on my behalf. I have never seen a barrel of oil, owned one, bought one, sold one . . .'

[2] John Burdon Sanderson (J. B. S.) Haldane (1892–1964): British, later Indian, scientist and statistician.

there's a tremendous amount of uncertainty. That's the whole distinction. The believer has to say, not just that there is a God – the Deist position that there may be a mind at work in the universe, a proposition we can't disprove – but that they *know* that mind.

HARRIS: Exactly.

HITCHENS: And can interpret it. They're on good terms with it. They get occasional revelations from it. They get briefings from it. Now, any decent argument, any decent intellect, has to begin by excluding people who claim to know more than they can possibly know. You start off by saying, 'Well, that's wrong to begin with. Now, can we get on with it?' So, theism is gone in the first round. It's off the island. It's out of the show.

HARRIS: That's a footnote I wanted to add to what Dan was saying. Even if mystery is a bitter pill we have to swallow in the end and we are cognitively closed to the truth at some level, that still doesn't give any scope to theism.

DENNETT: Absolutely not, because it's just as closed to them as it is to—

HARRIS: Exactly. And yet they claim perfect inerrancy of revelation.

HITCHENS: And also, they can't be allowed to forget what they used to say when they were strong enough to get away with it. Which is, 'This is really true in every detail, and if you don't believe it—'

HARRIS: We'll kill you. [*Laughs*]

HITCHENS: We'll kill you, and it may take some days to kill you, but we will get the job done. They wouldn't have the power they have now, if they hadn't had the power they had then.

DENNETT: And you know, what you just said, Christopher, actually I think strikes terror, strikes anxiety, in a lot of religious hearts. Because it just hasn't been brought home to them that this move of theirs is just off limits. It's just not the game; you can't do that. And they've been taught all their lives that you *can* do that – that it's a legitimate way of conducting a discussion. And here suddenly we're just telling them, 'I'm sorry, that is not a move in this game. In fact, it is a disqualifying move.'

HARRIS: Precisely the move you can't be respected for making.

HITCHENS: Adumbrate the move for me a bit, if you would. Say what you think that move is.

DENNETT: Somebody plays the faith card. They say, 'Look, I am a Christian, and we Christians, we just have to believe this, and that's it.' At which point – and I think this is the polite way of saying it – you say, 'Well, OK, if that's true, you'll just have to excuse yourself from the discussion, because you've declared yourself incompetent to proceed with an open mind.'

HITCHENS: OK, that's what I hoped you were saying.

DENNETT: If you really can't defend your view, then, sorry, you can't put it forward. We're not going to let you play the faith card. Now, if you want to defend what your Holy Book says in terms that we can appreciate, fine. But because it says it in the Holy Book – that just doesn't cut any ice at all. And if you think it does, you're clearly – first of all, that's just arrogant. It is a bullying move, and we're just not going to accept it.

HARRIS: And it's a move that *they* don't accept, when done in the name of another faith.

DENNETT: Exactly.

HITCHENS: In which case, could I ask you something – all three of you, who are wiser than I on this matter. What do we think of Victor Stenger's book that says we cannot scientifically disprove the existence of God?[1] Do you have a view of this?

DENNETT: Which God? I haven't read the book.

---

[1] Victor Stenger (1935–2014): US particle physicist, philosopher and popular science writer. Works include *God: The Failed Hypothesis. How Science Shows that God Does Not Exist* (New York: Prometheus, 2007), in which he came as close as anyone has done to saying that the existence of God has been disproved.

HITCHENS: Any. Either a creating one or a supervising one, and certainly an intervening one – I think that's fairly exhaustive. My view has always been that since we have to live with uncertainty, only those who are certain [should] leave the room before the discussion can become adult. Victor Stenger seems to think that now we've got to the stage where we can say with reasonable confidence that it is disproved. Or that it's not vindicated. I just thought it would be an interesting proposition. Because it matters a lot to me that our opinions are congruent with uncertainty.

HARRIS: I think the weakest link is this foundational claim about the texts – this idea that we know the Bible to be the perfect word of an omniscient deity. That is an especially weak claim. And it really is their epistemological gold standard. It all rests on that. If the Bible isn't a magic book, Christianity evaporates. If the Qur'an isn't a magic book, Islam evaporates. And when you look at the books and ask yourself, 'Is there the slightest shred of evidence that this is the product of omniscience? Is there a single sentence in here that couldn't have been uttered by a person for whom a wheelbarrow would have been emergent technology?' you have to say no. If the Bible had an account of DNA and electricity and other things that would astonish us, then OK, our jaws would drop and we'd have to have a sensible conversation about the source of this knowledge.

HITCHENS: Dinesh D'Souza[1] – by the way, one of the much more literate and well-read and educated of our antagonists; I'm going to be debating him soon – makes this statement in his new book:[2] He says that in Genesis, which people used to mock, it says, 'Let there be light,' and then only a few staves later you get the sun and the moon and the stars. How could that be? Well, that's actually, according to the big bang, that would be right.

DAWKINS: Yes, but that's not impressive.

HITCHENS: The bang precedes the galaxies, believe me. [*Laughter*]

HARRIS: Well, I try to demonstrate this cast of mind in a very long endnote in *The End of Faith* where I show that with the eyes of faith, you can discover magical prescience in any text. I literally walked into the cookbook aisle of a bookstore, randomly opened a cookbook, found a recipe for, I think it was, wok-seared shrimp with ogo relish or something, and then came up with a mystical interpretation of the recipe. Anyone can do this. You can play connect-the-dots with any crazy text and find wisdom in it.

---

[1] Dinesh D'Souza (b. 1961): US Indian political commentator, writer and film-maker; president of The King's College, a Christian school in New York, 2010–12.

[2] Dinesh D'Souza, *What's So Great About Christianity* (Washington DC: Regnery, 2007).

HITCHENS: Well, Michael Shermer[1] did that with the Bible Code, hidden messages in the Bible. Very, very good. You can absolutely write yesterday's headlines from it, any time you like.

HARRIS: I have a question for the three of you. Is there any argument *for* faith? Any challenge to your atheism that has given you pause? That has set you back on your heels, where you felt you didn't have a ready answer?

DENNETT: [*Laughs*] I can't think of any.

DAWKINS: I think the closest is the idea that the fundamental constants of the universe are too good to be true. And that does seem to me to need some kind of explanation if it's true. Victor Stenger doesn't think it is true, but many physicists do. It certainly doesn't in any way suggest to me a creative intelligence, because you're still left with the problem of explaining where *that* came from. And a creative intelligence who is sufficiently creative and intelligent enough to fine-tune the constants of the universe to give rise to us has got to be a lot more fine-tuned himself than—

HITCHENS: Why create all the other planets in our solar system dead? [*Laughs*]

---

[1] Michael Shermer (b. 1954): US science writer and historian of science; founder of the Skeptics Society. For 'Michael Shermer decodes the Bible Code' (23 July 2007), see https://www.youtube.com/watch?v=Lk3VgQgxiqE.

DAWKINS: Well, that's a separate question.

HITCHENS: Bishop Montefiore[1] was very good at this –
he was a friend of mine. He said you had to marvel at
the conditions for life and the knife edge on which they
are, as though it is a knife edge. Yes, our planet is, a lot
of it, too hot or too cold.

HARRIS: Right, and riddled with parasites.

HITCHENS: And it's completely too hot or too cold, as it
were, and that's just one solar system, the only one we
know about where there is life. Not much of a designer.
And, of course, you can't get out of the infinite regress.
But no, I've not come across a single persuasive argument of that kind. But I wouldn't have expected to,
because, as I realized when I thought one evening, they
never come up with anything new. Well, why would
they? Their arguments are very old by definition. And
they were all evolved when we knew very, very little
about the natural order.

  The only argument that I find at all attractive – and
this is for faith as well as for theism – is what I suppose
I would call the apotropaic, when people say, 'All
praise belongs to God for this. He's to be thanked for
all this.' That is actually a form of modesty – it's a
superstitious one. That's why I say 'apotropaic'. But

---

[1] Hugh Montefiore (1920–2005): English Anglican priest and
theologian; Bishop of Kingston, 1970–8; Bishop of Birmingham,
1978–1987.

it's avoiding hubris. It's also, for that reason, obviously pre-monotheistic. Religion does, or can, help people to avoid hubris, I think, morally and intellectually.

DAWKINS: But that's not an argument that it's true.

HITCHENS: No, no. There aren't, and cannot be, any such arguments.

HARRIS: Well, maybe I should broaden this question.

DENNETT: No, no, wait a minute. I can give you several discoveries which would shake my faith right to the ground.

HITCHENS: Rabbits in the Precambrian.[1]

DAWKINS: No, no, no.

HARRIS: I'm looking for an argument not so much for the plausibility of religious belief but one that suggests that what we're up to – criticizing faith – is a bad thing.

DAWKINS: Oh, that's much easier. Somebody could come up with an argument that says that the world is a better place if everybody believes a falsehood.

DENNETT: Oh, that. Yes.

HARRIS: Is there any context in your work or in dialogue with your critics where you feel that such an argument has given you pause?

---

[1] Said to have been J. B. S. Haldane's response when asked what could shake his belief in evolution.

DENNETT: Oh, yes. Oh, yes. Not so much in *Breaking the Spell*, but when I was working on my book on free will, *Freedom Evolves*, I kept running into critics who were basically expressing something very close to a religious view – namely, free will is such an important idea that if we gave up the idea of free will, people would lose the sense of responsibility and we would have chaos. And you really don't want to look too closely. Just avert your eyes; do not look too closely at this issue of free will and determinism. And I thought about that explicitly in the environmental-impact category. OK, could I imagine that my irrepressible curiosity could lead me to articulate something, true or false, which would have such devastating effects on the world that I should just shut up and change the subject? I think that's a good question, which we all should ask – absolutely! I spent a lot of time thinking hard about that, and I wouldn't have published either of those two books if I hadn't come to the conclusion that it was not only, as it were, environmentally safe to proceed this way but obligatory. I think you *should* ask that question. I do.

DAWKINS: Before publishing a book, but not before deciding for yourself, 'Do I think that this is true or not?' One should never do what some politically motivated critics often do, which is to say, 'This is so politically obnoxious that it cannot be true.'

DENNETT: Oh, yes.

DAWKINS: Which is a different—

DENNETT: Which is a different thing entirely. No, no.

HITCHENS: It would be like discovering that you thought the bell curve on white and black intelligence was a correct interpretation of IQ. You could say, 'Now what am I going to do?' Fortunately, these questions don't, in fact, present themselves in that way.

HARRIS: I'll tell you one place where it's presented itself to me. I think it was an op-ed in the *L.A. Times* – I could be mistaken. But someone argued that the reason the Muslim population in the US isn't radicalized the way it is in western Europe is largely the result of the fact that we honour faith so much in our discourse that the community has not become as insular and as grievance-ridden as it has in western Europe. Now, I don't know if that's true, but if it were true, that could give me a moment's pause.

HITCHENS: That would be of interest. James Wolfensohn,[1] lately of the World Bank, recently the negotiator on Gaza, says he firmly believes that he had tremendous influence for good with the Muslim Brotherhood and Hamas because he was an Orthodox Jew. If so, I think it would be disgusting – and he shouldn't have had the job in the first place. Because we know one absolute

---

[1] James Wolfensohn (b. 1933): Australian American lawyer, financier and economist; president of the World Bank Group, 1995–2005; UN/Quartet special envoy for Gaza disengagement, 2005–6.

thing for certain about that conflict, which is that it's been made infinitely worse by the monotheisms. If it were only a national and territorial dispute, it would have been solved by now. But his self-satisfaction in saying so, even if it were true, would turn me even more against him.

PART II

Harris: Two issues converge here. One is the question, 'What do we want to accomplish?' What do we reasonably think we can accomplish? And then there's this article of faith that circulates, unfortunately, even among people of our viewpoint, that you can't argue anyone out of their beliefs.

So is this a completely fatuous exercise? Or can we actually win a war of ideas with people? Judging from my e-mail, we can. I'm constantly getting e-mail from people who have lost their faith and were, in effect, argued out of it. And the straw that broke that camel's back was either one of our books, or some other process of reasoning, or the incompatibility between what they knew to be true and what they were told by their faith. I think we have to highlight the fact that it's possible for people to be shown the contradictions internal to their faith, or the contradiction between their faith and what we've come to know to be true about the universe. The process can take minutes or months or years, but they have to renounce their superstition in the face of what they now know to be true.

DAWKINS: I was having an argument with a very sophisticated biologist who's a brilliant expositor of evolution and still believes in God.[1] I said, 'How can you? What's this all about?' And he said, 'I accept all your rational arguments. However, it's faith.' And then he said this very significant phrase to me: 'There's a reason that it's called faith!' He said it very decisively, very – almost – aggressively: 'There's a reason that it's called faith.' And that was, to him, the absolute knock-down clincher. You can't argue with it, because it's faith. And he said it proudly and defiantly, rather than in any sort of apologetic way.

HITCHENS: Well, you get it all the time in North America from people who say you've got to read William James[2] and to be able to judge other people's subjective experiences, which is something that's by definition impossible to do. 'If it's real to them, why can't you respect it?' This wouldn't be accepted in any other

---

[1] Kenneth R. Miller (b. 1948), professor of biology and Royce Professor for Teaching Excellence, Brown University.

[2] William James (1842–1910): US philosopher and psychologist; author of *The Varieties of Religious Experience* (New York: Longmans, Green & Co., 1902).

field of argument at all. The impression people are under is the critical thing about them.

I had a debate with a very senior Presbyterian in Orange County. I asked him – because we were talking about biblical literalism, of which he wasn't an exponent – but I asked him, 'Well, what about the graves opening at the time of the Crucifixion, according to Matthew? And everyone getting out of their graves in Jerusalem and walking around greeting old friends in the city?' I was going to ask him, 'Doesn't that rather cheapen the idea of the Resurrection of Jesus?' But he mistook my purpose: he thought I wanted to know if he *believed* that had happened. And he said that as a historian, which he also was, he was inclined to doubt it, but that as a Presbyterian minister he thought it was true. Well, all right then. See, for me, it was enough that I got him to say that. I said, 'In that case, I rest my case. I don't want to say any more to you now. You've said all I could say.'

HARRIS: Well, there's one other chip I'd like to put on the table here. There's the phenomenon of someone like Francis Collins, or the biologist you just mentioned – someone who obviously has enough of the facts on board, and enough of a scientific education, to know better and still does not know better, or professes not to know better.

I think we have a cultural problem here. This was brought home to me at one talk I gave. A physics professor came up to me at the end of the talk and told me that he had brought one of his graduate students who was a devout Christian and who was quite shaken by my talk, and all I got of this report was that this was the first time his faith had ever been explicitly challenged. So it's apparently true to say that you can go through the curriculum of becoming a scientist and never have your faith challenged, because it's taboo to do so.

And now we have engineers in the Muslim world who can build nuclear bombs and who still think it's plausible that you can get to paradise and get seventy-two virgins. And we have people like Francis Collins who think that on Sunday you can kneel down in the dewy grass and give yourself to Jesus because you're in the presence of a frozen waterfall, and on Monday you can be a physical geneticist.

HITCHENS: Well, according to our friend Pervez Hoodbhoy,[1] the great Pakistani physicist, there are people who think you can use the jinns, the devils, and harness their power for a reactor.

HARRIS: It's almost tempting to fund such a project.

DENNETT: I think it may be easier than we're supposing to shake people's faith. There's been a moratorium on this for a long time. We're just the beginning of a new

---

[1] Pervez Hoodbhoy (b. 1950): Pakistani nuclear physicist; promoter of free speech, education and secularism in Pakistan.

wave of explicit attempts to shake people's faith, and it's bearing fruit. And the obstacles, it seems to me, are not that we don't have the facts or the arguments. It's the strategic reasons for not professing it, not admitting it, not admitting it to yourself, not admitting it in public because your family's going to view it as a betrayal. You're just embarrassed to admit that you were taken in by this for so long.

It takes, I think, tremendous courage to just declare that you've given that all up. And if we can find ways to help people find that courage and give them some examples of people who have done this and they're doing just fine – they may have lost the affections of a parent or something like that. They may have hurt some family members – but still I think it's a good thing to encourage them. I don't think we should assume that we can't do this. I think we can.

DAWKINS: Yes, and it's almost patronizing to suggest that we couldn't. On the other hand, I think we all know people who seem to manage this kind of split-brain feat of, as Sam says, believing one thing on a Sunday and then something totally contradictory, or incompatible, in the rest of the week. And there's nothing, I suppose, neurologically wrong with that; there's no reason why one shouldn't have a brain that's split in that kind of way.

DENNETT: But it is unstable in a certain way. And I'm sure you're right that people do this, and they're very good at it. And they do it by deflecting attention from it. Let's start focusing attention—

DAWKINS: But how can you live with a contradiction in your—?

DENNETT: By forgetting that you're doing this and by not attending to it. I think what I would love to do is to invent a memorable catchphrase or term that would rise unbidden in their minds when they caught themselves doing that. And then they would think, 'Oh, this is one of those cosmic shifts that Dennett and Dawkins and Harris and Hitchens are talking about. Oh, right! And they think this is somehow illicit.' Just to create a little more awareness in them of what a strange thing it is that they're doing.

HITCHENS: I'm afraid to say that I think that cognitive dissonance is probably necessary for everyday survival. Everyone does it a bit.

DENNETT: You mean tolerating cognitive dissonance?

HITCHENS: No, practising it. Take the case of someone who's a member of MoveOn.org.[1] They think the United States government is a brutal, militaristic, imperial regime. It crushes the poor and invades other people's countries. But they pay their taxes, and it's very, very rare that they don't. They send their children to [public] school. They do their stuff. You know,

---

[1] US progressive public policy advocacy group, formed in 1998.

they don't act all the time as if 10 per cent of what they believe is true. Partly because it would be impossible. Say, with people in the 1950s, members of the John Birch Society, who thought President Eisenhower was a communist. OK? You get up in the morning, you believe that: the White House is run by the Kremlin. But then you have to go and get the groceries, and do all that stuff.

HARRIS: Too many commitments. Yes.

DAWKINS: You still have to go and do it.

HITCHENS: But you absolutely wouldn't be challengeable in your belief. It'd be very, very important to you. But there'd be no way in your life, your real life, of vindicating or practising the opinion that you have. And I'm sure that the same is true of people who say, 'Well, I shouldn't really prefer one child to another, or one parent to another, but I do. I'm just not going to act as if I do.' All kinds of things like this. Senator Craig[1] saying he's not gay. Thinking in his own mind that he's absolutely sure he's not, but he can't manage his life by saying he is or he isn't.

So, a question I wanted to ask was this. We should ask ourselves what our real objective is. Do we in fact

---

[1] Larry Craig (b. 1945): former US Republican Senator for Idaho (1991–2009). Arrested for 'lewd conduct' in June 2007; subsequently pleaded guilty to a lesser charge of 'disorderly conduct'; stated that he was not, nor ever had been, gay.

wish to see a world without faith? I think I would have to say that I don't. I don't either expect to, or wish to, see that.

HARRIS: What do you mean by faith?

HITCHENS: Faith, as often as it's cut down or superseded or discredited, replicates, it seems to me, extraordinarily fast, I think for Freudian reasons – principally to do with the fear of extinction or annihilation.

HARRIS: You mean faith in supernatural paradigms?

HITCHENS: Yes. Wish thinking. And then the other thing is: would I want this argument to come to an end, with all having conceded, 'Hitchens really won that round. Now nobody in the world believes in God'?

Now, apart from being unable to picture this, [*Laughter*] I'm not even completely certain that it's what I want. I think it is rather to be considered the foundation of all arguments about epistemology, philosophy, biology, and so on – that it's the thing you have to always be arguing against. The other explanation.

DAWKINS: I find that an extraordinary thing to say. I don't understand what you're saying. I mean, I understand you're saying that it will never work, but I don't understand why you wouldn't wish it.

HITCHENS: Because – I think, a bit like the argument between Huxley[1] and Wilberforce[2] or Darrow[3] and William Jennings Bryan – I want it to go on.

DAWKINS: Because it's interesting.

HITCHENS: I want our side to get more refined and theirs to be ever more exposed. But I can't see [this happening] with one hand clapping.

HARRIS: You don't want it to go on with the jihadists?

HITCHENS: No, but I don't have a difference of opinion with the jihadists.

HARRIS: Well, you do, in terms of the legitimacy of their project.

HITCHENS: No, not really. There's nothing to argue about with that. I mean, there it's a simple matter: I want them to be extirpated. That's a purely primate response with me – recognizing the need to destroy an enemy in order to assure my own survival. I have no

[1] Thomas Henry Huxley (1825–95): English biologist and champion of Darwinian evolution, notably at the 1860 debate on the subject held by the British Association in Oxford, where he spoke in opposition to Samuel Wilberforce.

[2] Samuel Wilberforce (1805–73): Anglican cleric; Bishop of Oxford from 1845; took part in the 1860 debate on evolution, opposing Darwin's assertion that humans and apes shared common ancestors.

[3] Clarence Darrow (1857–1938): US lawyer; defended the teacher John Scopes in the 'Scopes trial' of 1925, in opposition to Bryan.

interest at all in what they think. We haven't yet come to your question about Islam, but I have no interest at all in what jihadists think. I'm only interested in refining methods of destroying them. A task for which, by the way, one gets very little secular support.

HARRIS: Yes, that's notable.

HITCHENS: Most atheists don't want this fight. The most important one is the one they want to shirk. They'd far rather go off and dump on Billy Graham.[1] Because on that, they know that there's no danger.

DENNETT: I think that because we find the idea of exterminating these people is abhorrent, and we think that besides, it will—

HITCHENS: No, I said 'extirpating'.

DENNETT: Extirpate.

HITCHENS: Complete destruction of the jihadist forces. Extermination, I think, applies more to a species.

DAWKINS: But, Christopher, going back to your point: It sounds as though you like argument. You like having – it's almost the theatre of having – an intellectual argument, which would be lost.

---

[1] Billy Graham (1918–2018): US Southern Baptist minister and evangelist, renowned for the large indoor and outdoor rallies at which he preached.

HITCHENS: Well, I would rather say 'the dialectic', Richard. In other words, one learns from arguing with other people. And I think all of us around this table have probably enhanced or improved our own capacities as reasoners in this context.

DAWKINS: But there are plenty of other things to reason about. Having won the battle against religion, we can go back to science or whatever it is we practise, and we can argue and reason about that. And there's plenty of arguments, that are really worthwhile arguments, to be had.

HITCHENS: It will always be the case that some will attribute their presence here to the laws of biology and others will attribute their presence here to a divine plan that has a scheme for them.

DAWKINS: Well, that's what—

HITCHENS: You can tell a lot, in my view, about people from which of these views they take. And as we all know, only one of those views makes sense. But how do we know that? Because we have to contrast it with the opposite one, which is not going to disappear.

HARRIS: Let me make an analogy here. You could have said the same thing about witchcraft at some point in recent history.

HITCHENS: Yes.

HARRIS: You could say that every culture has had a belief in witches, a belief in the efficacy of magic spells, witchcraft is just ubiquitous and we're never going to get rid of it, and we're fools to try. Or we can try only as a matter of dialectic, but witchcraft is going to be with us for ever. And yet witchcraft has vanished, almost without exception. I mean you can find certain communities where—

HITCHENS: Not at all. Not at all. Witchcraft is completely ineradicable and spreads like weeds, often under animists and Christians.

DENNETT: Not in the Western world.

HARRIS: I mean frank witchcraft. The witchcraft of the evil eye, and instead of medicine you have—

HITCHENS: You think you've got rid of that?

HARRIS: Fundamentally, we've gotten rid of that. Yes.

DAWKINS: In any case, don't you want to get rid of it?

HITCHENS: There's currently a campaign to get Wiccans registered to be buried in Arlington Cemetery.

HARRIS: I'm talking about a willingness to kill your neighbours because you think there's some causal mechanism by which they, through their evil intent, could have destroyed your crops psychically, or cast an evil eye upon your child. This comes with ignorance of medical science.

HITCHENS: Yes, it does.

HARRIS: You don't know why people get sick, and you suspect your neighbour of ill intent, and then witchcraft fills the void there.

HITCHENS: I wouldn't say in such a case that one didn't wish to be without it, that we've lost something interesting to argue with.

HARRIS: But we're not dealing with the claims of witches intruding upon medical practices. Don't go to alternative medicine and acupuncture here. I'm talking about real witchcraft, medieval witchcraft.

HITCHENS: Actually I was about to do that very thing. And the *Washington Post* publishes horoscopes every day.

HARRIS: Astrology is yet another matter.

DENNETT: Yes, but astrology is a pale—

HITCHENS: Let's take them out of it. Astrology is not going to be eradicated.

DENNETT: OK. Well, but it doesn't need to be eradicated.

DAWKINS: But you're confusing whether it's going to be eradicated and whether you want it to be eradicated. And it sounds as though you *don't* want it to be eradicated, because you want something to argue against. And something to sharpen your wits on.

HITCHENS: Yes, I think that is in fact what I want.

DENNETT: But in fact, instead of thinking about eradication, why not think about it the way an evolutionary epidemiologist would, and say, 'What we want to do is encourage the evolution of avirulence. We want to get rid of the harmful kind. I don't care about astrology – I don't think it's harmful enough. I mean, it was a little scary when Reagan was reportedly using astrology to make decisions, but that, I hope, anomalous case aside, I find the superstition that astrology is important to be relatively harmless. If we could only relegate the other enthusiasms to the status of astrology, I'd be happy.

HITCHENS: Well, look, you don't like my answer. But I think the question should be – it is going to be asked of us; it was asked of me today, actually, on TV. They said, 'Do you wish no one was going to church this morning in the United States?'

DENNETT: What's your answer?

HITCHENS: Well, I've given mine, and Richard has disagreed. But the answer I gave this morning was that I think people would be much better off without false consolation, and I don't want them trying to inflict their beliefs on me. They'd be doing themselves and me a favour if they gave it up. So perhaps in that sense I contradict myself. I mean, I wish they would stop it, but then I would be left with no one to argue with. And I certainly didn't say that I thought if they would only listen to me they'd stop going, OK? So, there are two questions here.

But I'd love to hear: would you like to say that you look forward to a world where no one has any faith?

DAWKINS: Yes, I want to answer this. Whether it's astrology or religion or anything else, I want to live in a world where people think sceptically for themselves, look at evidence. Not because astrology's harmful; I guess it probably isn't harmful. But if you go through the world thinking that it's OK to just believe things because you believe them without evidence, then you're missing so much. And it's such a wonderful experience to live in the world and understand *why* you're living in the world, and understand what makes it work, understand about the real stars, understand about astronomy, that it's an impoverishing thing to be reduced to the pettiness of astrology.

And I think you can say the same of religion. The universe is a grand, beautiful, wonderful place, and it's petty and parochial and cheapening to believe in jinns and supernatural creators and supernatural interferers. I think you could make an aesthetic case that you'd want to get rid of faith.

HITCHENS: I could not possibly agree with you more.

DENNETT: But let's talk about priorities. If we could just get rid of some of the most pernicious and noxious excesses, what would be the triumphs you would go for first? What would really thrill you as an objective reached? Let's look at Islam. And let's look at Islam as realistically as we can. Is there any remote chance of a reformed, reasonable Islam?

DAWKINS: Well, the present savage Islam is actually rather recent, isn't it?

DENNETT: You have to go back quite a way, I think, to get the—

HARRIS: Only up to a point. And again, whether or not we're equipped to deliver it, we're not the most persuasive mouthpieces for this criticism. It takes someone like Ayaan Hirsi Ali,[1] or a Muslim scholar, someone like Ibn Warraq,[2] to authentically criticize Islam and have it be heard by people, especially the secular liberals of the sort who don't trust our take on this. But it seems to me that you have distinct historical periods in the history of Islam. You have a caliphate, or a Muslim country where Islam reigns and is unmolested from the outside, and then Islam can be as totalitarian and happy with itself as possible, and you don't see the inherent liabilities of its creed. The political scientist

[1] Ayaan Hirsi Ali (b. 1969): Dutch American scholar and activist; born in Somalia; vocal critic of Islam and advocate of the rights of Muslim women. See p. 2 above.

[2] The pen name of an anonymous critic of Islam; one of the founders in 1998 of the Institute for the Secularisation of Islamic Society.

Samuel Huntington[1] said, 'Islam has bloody borders.' It's at the borders that we're noticing this problem; it's at the borders of Islam and modernity. There is a conflict between Islam and modernity. But, yes, you can find instances in the history of Islam where people weren't running around waging jihad, because they had *successfully* waged jihad.

DENNETT: But what about women in that world?

DAWKINS: Exactly. The suffering of women within those borders.

DENNETT: Even in the best of times.

HARRIS: Of course.

HITCHENS: But there's obviously some kind of syncretism. We know quite a lot now. There have been some wonderful books, María Menocal's book on Andalucía, for example,[2] – on periods when Islamic civilization was relatively at peace with its neighbours and doing a lot of work of its own on matters that were not jihadist. And I saw, myself, during the wars post-Yugoslavia, the Bosnian Muslims behaving far better than the

---

[1] Samuel Huntington (1927–2008): US political scientist and presidential adviser; propounded in 1993 his theory of 'the clash of civilizations', presented in book form as *The Clash of Civilizations and the Remaking of World Order* (1996).

[2] María Rosa Menocal, *The Ornament of the World: How Muslims, Jews and Christians Created a Culture of Tolerance in Medieval Spain* (Boston: Little, Brown, 2002).

Christians, either Catholic or Orthodox. They were the victims of religious massacres and not the perpetrators of them, and they were the ones who believed the most in multiculturalism. So it *can* happen. You could even meet people who said they were atheist Muslims, or Muslim atheists.

DENNETT: Wow!

HITCHENS: In Sarajevo, you could, yes. Which is a technical impossibility. But the problem is this, whether we think, as I certainly very firmly do believe, that totalitarianism is innate in all religion because it has to want an absolute, unchallengeable, eternal authority.

DENNETT: In all religions.

HITCHENS: Must be so. The Creator whose will can't be challenged. Our comments on his will are unimportant. His will is absolute, and applies after we're dead as well as before we're born. That is the origin of totalitarianism. I think Islam states that in the most alarming way, in that it comes as the third of the monotheisms and says: 'Nothing further is required. This is the last. There have been previous words from God; we admit that. We don't claim to be exclusive, but we do claim to be final. There's no need for any further work on this point.'

HARRIS: 'And we do claim that there is no distance between theology and civil matters.'

HITCHENS: That is the worst thing in our world. In our world, surely the worst thing that anyone can say is, 'No further inquiries needed. You've already got all you need to know. All else is commentary.' That is the *most* sinister and dangerous thing, and that is a claim Islam makes that others don't make in quite the same way.

DENNETT: Well, let me play devil's advocate for a moment on that point.

HITCHENS: There's no regard for Islam in Christianity or Judaism, but there is [regard for these other faiths] in Islam. They accept all the bits of Judaism. They love Abraham and his willingness to sacrifice his son. They love all that. They absolutely esteem the Virgin Birth, the most nonsensical bits of Christianity. They think all that is great. 'You're all welcome to join, but we have the final word.' That's deadly. And I think our existence is incompatible with that preaching.

DENNETT: Let me just play devil's advocate for a moment, so at least we're clear what the position is.

HITCHENS: I'd rather speak for the devil pro bono myself. [*Laughter*]

DENNETT: We can all speak for the devil. I'm sure a lot of people think we're doing just that.

I, for one, think that the fact that something is true is not quite sufficient for spreading it about, or for trying to discover it. The idea that there are things that we should just not try to find out is an idea that I take seriously. And I think we at least have to examine the proposition that there's such a thing as knowing more than is good for us.

Now, if you accept that so far, then a possibility we have to take seriously – even when we reject it, we should reject it having taken it seriously – is the Muslim idea that indeed the West has simply gone way too far, that there's lots of knowledge that isn't good for us. It's knowledge that we were better off without. And the fact is that many Muslims would like to turn the clock back. They can't, of course. But I have a certain sympathy for a Muslim who says, 'Well, yeah, the cat's out of the bag. It's too late. It's a tragedy. You in the West have exposed truths to yourselves, and now you're forcing them on us – truths that the species would be better off not knowing.'

HITCHENS: I'm absolutely riveted by what you say. I'd really love an instance, in theory or practice, of something you think we could know but could forbid ourselves to know. Because that is harder for me to imagine in a world without faith, I must say.

HARRIS: Well, you brought up the bell curve. If there were reliable differences in intelligence between races or genders—

HITCHENS: But I don't think any of us here do think that that's the case. You must have thought of something you could believe but wish you didn't know.

DENNETT: Oh, I don't think it's hard to dream up things which, if they were true, it might be better for the human race to go on not knowing them.

HITCHENS: Could you concretize it just a little more? I'm completely fascinated.

DAWKINS: The hypothetical is one thing. But Christopher's asking, 'Have you ever suppressed something that—?'

HITCHENS: Was there something you had in mind?

DENNETT: No. No, I haven't.

DAWKINS: No.

HITCHENS: Can you imagine yourself doing so, by the way? I can't.

DENNETT: Oh, I can imagine it. I hope it never comes up.

HARRIS: Take the synthesizing of bioweapons. Should *Nature* publish the recipe for smallpox?

DENNETT: Yes, exactly. There's all those—

HITCHENS: Well, all right. But that wouldn't be a knowledge of which we should remain innocent. That would be more like a capacity.

HARRIS: Certainly you can conceive of a circumstance where someone can seek knowledge the only conceivable application of which would be unethical, or the dissemination of which would put power in the wrong hands. But, actually, you brought up something which I think is crucial here. Because it's not so much the spread of seditious truths to Islam or to the rest of the world that I think we're guilty of in the eyes of our opponents. It's that we don't honour facts that aren't easily quantified or easily discussed in science. The classic retort to all of us is, 'Prove to me that you love your wife' – as though this were a knock-down argument against atheism: you can't prove it. Well, if you unpack that a little bit, you *can* prove it. You can demonstrate it. We know what we mean by 'love'. But there is this domain of the sacred that is not easily captured by science, and scientific discourse has ceded it to religious discourse.

DENNETT: Well, and artistic discourse.

HARRIS: Yes.

DENNETT: Which is not religious, necessarily.

HARRIS: But I would argue it's not even well captured by art, in the same way that love is not well captured by art. And compassion isn't. You can represent them in art, but they're not reducible to art. You don't go into the museum and find compassion in its purest form. And I think there's something about the way we, as atheists, merely dismiss the bogus claims of religious people that convinces religious people that there's something we're missing. And I think we have to be sensitive to this.

HITCHENS: Absolutely. That's why they bring up the argument about when has secularism ever built anything like Durham Cathedral or Chartres, or produced devotional painting or the music of—

DENNETT: Bach.

HITCHENS: I guess it would have to be Bach, yes.

HARRIS: But I think we have answers to that.

HITCHENS: Yes, we do.

HARRIS: And you provide a very good answer: If there had been secular patronage of the arts at that point, then (1) we can't know that Michelangelo was actually a believer, because the consequences of professing your unbelief back then was death. And (2), if we had a secular organization to commission Michelangelo, we would have all that secular artwork.

HITCHENS: I didn't actually say that the corollary held.

HARRIS: Which?

HITCHENS: I think it's true that we can't know, with devotional painting and sculpture, whether the patronage did or didn't have a lot to do with it. But I can't hear myself saying, 'If only you had a secular painter, he would have done work just as good.' I don't know why – and I'm quite happy to find that I don't know why – I can't quite hear myself saying it.

DAWKINS: What? That Michelangelo, if he'd been commissioned to do the ceiling of a museum of science, wouldn't have produced something just as wonderful?

HITCHENS: In some way, I'm reluctant to affirm that, yes.

DAWKINS: Really? I find it very, very easy to believe that.

HITCHENS: That could be a difference between us. I mean, with devotional poetry – I don't know very much about painting and architecture, and some of the devotional architecture, like, say, St Peter's, I don't like anyway and knowing that it was built by a special sale of indulgences doesn't help, either. With devotional poetry, like, let us say, John Donne[1] or George Herbert,[2] I find it very hard to imagine that it's faked or done for a patron.

DAWKINS: Yes, I think that's fair enough.

HITCHENS: It would be very improbable that people wrote poetry like that to please anyone.

DAWKINS: But in any case, what conclusion would you draw? If Donne's devotional poetry is wonderful, so what? That doesn't show that it represents truth in any sense.

---

[1] John Donne (1572–1631): English poet and cleric; Dean of St Paul's Cathedral from 1612; wrote both secular and religious poetry and prose.

[2] George Herbert (1593–1633): Welsh poet and cleric; Canon of Lincoln Cathedral from 1626.

HITCHENS: Not in the least. My favourite devotional poem is Philip Larkin's 'Church Going'.[1] One of the best poems ever written. It exactly expresses . . . I wish I had it here; well, actually I do have it here; if you like I can read it. But I wouldn't trust anyone who believed any more, or any less, than Larkin does when he goes to a wayside Gothic church in the English countryside. Who felt – I don't say 'believed'; I shouldn't say 'believed' – who felt any more than he does. He's an atheist. Or who felt any less. There's something serious about this poem. And something written into the human personality as well as the landscape. But it goes without saying that it says nothing about the truth of religion.

DENNETT: I don't see how this is anything other than a special case. Other special cases of which would be that you just couldn't – I can't think of a perfect example – Only by being lost at sea for two years in a boat, say, and surviving, that's the only way you could conceivably write an account of that. It could not be fiction. And it's glorious, wonderful art. And it's *right*. That can be true, and we just accept it. That's true. And Donne's poetry: only very extreme circumstances could make it possible, and we can be grateful, perhaps, that those extreme circumstances existed and made it possible.

---

[1] Philip Larkin (1922–85): English poet and writer; librarian of Hull University from 1955. 'Church Going' appears in his 1955 volume *The Less Deceived*.

HARRIS: In his case, yes. But you wouldn't recommend being lost at sea to everyone.

DENNETT: No, no.

HITCHENS: No. I wouldn't recommend the worldview in 'Death Be Not Proud'[1] to anyone, either. The sonnet is wonderful, but it's complete gibberish if you look only at the words. It's the most extraordinary gibberish, if you look only at the words. But there's an x factor involved, which I'm quite happy to both assume will persist and will need to be confronted.

HARRIS: Right. You raised this issue, though, of whether or not we would wish the churches empty on Sundays, and I think you were uncertain whether you would. And I think I would agree. I would want a different church. I would want a different ritual, motivated by different ideas. But I think there's a place for the sacred in our lives, but under some construal that doesn't presuppose any bullshit. I think there's a usefulness to seeking profundity as a matter of our attention.

HITCHENS: Sure.

HARRIS: And our neglect of this area, as atheists, at times makes even our craziest opponents seem wiser than we

---

[1] Also known as 'Sonnet X': poem by John Donne, part of the *Divine Meditations* sequence, composed in 1609 and first published (posthumously) in 1633.

are. And it takes someone like Sayyid Qutb,[1] who is as crazy as it gets – he was Osama bin Laden's favourite philosopher. He came out to Greeley, Colorado, around 1950 and spent a year in America and noticed that his American hosts were spending all their time gossiping about movie stars and trimming their hedges and coveting each other's automobiles, and he came to believe that America, or the West, was so trivial in its preoccupations and so materialistic that it had to be destroyed. Now, this shouldn't be construed as my giving any credence to his worldview, but he had a point. There *is* something trivial and horrible about the day-to-day fascinations of most people, most of the time. There *is* a difference between using your attention wisely, in a meaningful way, and perpetual distraction. And traditionally only religion has tried to enunciate that difference. And I think that's a lapse in our—

DAWKINS: I think you've made that point, and we've accepted it, Sam. Going back to the thing about whether we'd like to see churches empty: I think I *would* like to see churches empty. What I wouldn't like to see, however, is ignorance of the Bible.

HITCHENS: No, very right!

DAWKINS: Because you cannot understand literature without knowing the Bible. You can't understand art,

[1] Sayyid Qutb (1906–66): Egyptian Islamic radical; leader of the Muslim Brotherhood.

you can't understand music, there are all sorts of things you can't understand, for historical reasons – but those historical reasons you can't wipe out. They're there. And so even if you don't actually go to church and pray, you've got to understand what it meant to people to pray, and why they did it, and what these verses in the Bible mean, and what this—

HARRIS: But is it only that? Just the historical appreciation of our ancestors' ignorance?

DAWKINS: You can more than just appreciate it. You can lose yourself in it, just as you can lose yourself in a work of fiction without actually believing that the characters are real.

DENNETT: But you're sure you want to see the churches empty? You can't imagine a variety of churches, maybe by their lights an extremely denatured church: a church which has rituals and loyalty and purpose and music, and they sing the songs and they do the rituals, but where the irrationality has simply been laundered out.

DAWKINS: Oh, OK, so you go to those places for funerals and weddings—

DENNETT: Yes, and also—

DAWKINS: —and you have beautiful poetry and music.

DENNETT: And also perhaps for—

DAWKINS: Group solidarity.

DENNETT: Group solidarity, to create some project which is hard to get off the ground otherwise.

HITCHENS: I think there's one more tiny thing. I haven't been tempted to go to church since I was a very small boy, but one reason that makes it very easy to keep me out of church is the use of the New English Bible.

DAWKINS: Oh, and how! Yes! [*Laughter*]

HITCHENS: There's really no point in going. I can't see how anyone does go, and I can see why people stay away. They've thrown away—

HARRIS: All the poetry. Yes.

HITCHENS: —a pearl richer than all their tribe.

DAWKINS: Absolutely.

HITCHENS: They don't even know what they've got. It's terrible. If I were a lapsed Catholic and I brooded about how I wanted my funeral to be, which is not something I'd—

DENNETT: You'd only want the Latin Mass.

HITCHENS: Yes!

DENNETT: Absolutely.

DAWKINS: But there's another issue there, which, of course, is that when it becomes intelligible, the nonsense becomes more transparent, and so if it's in Latin, it can survive much better. It's sort of like a camouflaged insect. It can get through the barriers because you can't see it. And when it's translated into not just English but modern English, you can see it for what it is.

DENNETT: But now, seriously: Do you therefore delight in the fact that churches are modernizing their texts and using the—

DAWKINS: No, I don't. It's an aesthetic point. No, I don't.

HITCHENS: That's the worst of both worlds.

DENNETT: That's what it seems to me. Yes.

HITCHENS: And we should be grateful for it. *We* didn't do this to them. [*Laughter*]

DENNETT: That's right. We didn't impose this on them, they did it to themselves.

HARRIS: We weren't clever enough.

HITCHENS: We don't blow up Shia mosques, either. We don't blow up the Bamiyan Buddhas. We don't desecrate. We would, for the reasons given by Sophocles in *Antigone*, have a natural resistance to profanity and desecration. We leave it to the pious to destroy churches and burn synagogues or blow up each other's mosques. And I think that's a point that we ought to, we might, spend more time making. Because I do think it is feared of us – which was my point to begin with – that we wish for a world that's somehow empty of this echo of music and poetry and the numinous, and so forth. That we would be happy in a Brave New World. And, since I don't think it's true of any of us—

DAWKINS: No. No, it's not.

DENNETT: No, definitely.

HITCHENS: I think it's a point we might spend a bit more time making. That the howling wilderness of nothingness is much more likely to result from holy war or religious conflict or theocracy than it is from a proper secularism, which would therefore I think, have to not just allow or leave or tolerate or condescend to or patronize but actually, in a sense, *welcome* the persistence of something like faith. I feel I've put it better now than I did at the beginning.

HARRIS: Well, what do you mean by 'something like faith'?

DENNETT: How like faith?

HITCHENS: Something like the belief that there must be more than we can know.

DENNETT: Well, that's fine.

HARRIS: Dan Dennett believes that. That's not faith.

DENNETT: Yes, sure!

HARRIS: We *know* there's more than we presently know and are likely to know.

HITCHENS: That was my original point in saying that if we could find a way of enforcing the distinction between the numinous and the superstitious, we would be doing something culturally quite important. Richard and I debated at the Methodist Central Hall with Scruton[1] and that rather weird team who kept on saying – Scruton, particularly – 'Well, what about good old Gothic spires,' and so forth. I said, 'Look, I wrote a book about the Parthenon. I'm intensely interested in it. I think everyone should go there, everyone should study it, and so forth. But everyone should abstain from the cult of Pallas Athena. Everyone should realize that probably what that beautiful sculptural frieze depicts may involve some human sacrifices. Athenian imperialism wasn't all that pretty, even in the Age of Pericles.' The great cultural project, in other words, may very well be to rescue what we have of the art and aesthetic of religion while discarding the supernatural.

DENNETT: And I think acknowledging the evil that was part of its creation in the first place. That is, we can't condone the beliefs and practices of the Aztecs, but we can stand in awe of, and want to preserve, their architecture and many other features of their culture. But not their practices [*laughs*] and not their beliefs.

DAWKINS: I was once a guest on a British radio programme called *Desert Island Discs*, where you have to choose

---

[1] Roger Scruton (b. 1944): English conservative philosopher and writer.

the eight records which you'd take to a desert island and talk about them. And one of the ones I chose was Bach's *Mache dich, mein Herze, rein*. Wonderful, wonderful sacred music.

DENNETT: Beautiful.

DAWKINS: And the woman questioning me couldn't understand why I would wish to have this piece of music. Beautiful music, and its beauty is indeed enhanced by knowing what it means. But you don't actually have to believe it; it's like reading fiction.

DENNETT: Exactly.

DAWKINS: You can lose yourself in fiction, and be totally moved to tears by it, but nobody would ever say you've got to believe that this person existed or that the sadness that you feel really reflected something that actually happened.

HITCHENS: Yes. Like the Irish bishop who said that he'd read *Gulliver's Travels* and for his part he didn't believe a word of it.[1] [*Laughter*] It's the best of *locus classicus*, I think – of all of that. Clearly, we're not cultural vandals, but maybe we should think about why so many people suspect that that's what we are. If I were to accept one criticism that these people make, or one suspicion that I suspect they harbour, or fear that they

---

[1] Letter from Jonathan Swift to Alexander Pope, 17 November 1726.

may have, I think that that might be the one: that it would be all chromium and steel and—

DENNETT: And no Christmas carols and no menorahs and no—

DAWKINS: Anybody who makes that criticism couldn't possibly have read any one of our books.

DENNETT: Well, that's another problem, too. And of course it isn't just our books, it's so many books. People don't read them. They just read the reviews, and they decide that's what the book is about.

HITCHENS: We're about to have the Christmas wars again, of course; this being the last day of September. You can feel it all coming on. But whenever it comes up, when I go on any of these shows to discuss it, I say it was Oliver Cromwell[1] who cut down the Christmas trees and forbade . . . It was the Puritan Protestants, the ancestors of the American fundamentalists, who said Christmas would be blasphemy.

DAWKINS: Yes. It's the Bamiyan Buddhas again.

HITCHENS: Do you at least respect your own traditions? Because I do. I think Cromwell was a great man in many other ways as well. Christmas is actually a pagan festival.

---

[1] Oliver Cromwell (1599–1658): English radical Protestant, soldier and politician; leader of Parliamentary forces in Civil Wars; Lord Protector of the English Commonwealth, 1653–8.

HARRIS: We were all outed with our Christmas trees last year.

DENNETT: Yes.

DAWKINS: I have not the slightest problem with Christmas trees.

DENNETT: We had our Christmas card, with our pictures of—

HITCHENS: It's a good old Norse booze-up. And why the hell not?

DENNETT: Well, but it's not just that.

HITCHENS: I like solstices as much as the next person.

DENNETT: We have an annual Christmas carol party, where we sing the music. And all the music with all the words, and not the secular Christmas stuff.

DAWKINS: And why not?

DENNETT: And it's just glorious stuff. That part of the Christian story is fantastic – it's just a beautiful tale! And you can love every inch of it without believing it.

DAWKINS: I once, at lunch, was next to the lady who was our opponent at that debate in London.

HITCHENS: Rabbi Neuberger.[1]

---

[1] Julia Neuberger (b. 1950): British rabbi and member of the House of Lords; senior rabbi of the West London Synagogue from 2011.

DAWKINS: Rabbi Neuberger. And she asked me whether I said grace in New College when I happened to be senior fellow. And I said, 'Of course I say grace. It's a matter of simple courtesy.' And she was furious that I should somehow be so hypocritical as to say grace. And I could only say, 'Well, look, it may mean something to you, but it means absolutely nothing to me. This is a Latin formula which has some history, and I appreciate history.' Freddie Ayer,[1] the philosopher, also used to say grace, and what he said was, 'I won't utter falsehoods but I have no objection to uttering meaningless statements.' [*Laughter*]

HITCHENS: That's very good. The Wykeham Professor.

DAWKINS: The Wykeham Professor, yes.

HITCHENS: Did we answer your question on Islam?

HARRIS: I don't know. Well, I'll ask a related question. Do you feel there's any burden we have, as critics of religion, to be evenhanded in our criticism of religion, or is it fair to notice that there's a spectrum of religious ideas and commitments and Islam is on one end of it and the Amish and the Jains and others are on another

---

[1] Alfred Jules Ayer (1910–89), known as A.J. or 'Freddie' Ayer: British philosopher; works include *Language, Truth and Logic* (1936), in which he propounded the 'verification principle'; Wykeham Professor of Logic at Oxford from 1959.

end, and there are real differences here that we have to take seriously.

DENNETT: Well, of course we have to take them seriously, but we don't have to do the network-balancing trick all the time. There are plenty of people taking care of pointing out the good stuff, and the benign stuff. And we can acknowledge that and then concentrate on the problems. That's what critics do. Again, if we were writing books about the pharmaceutical industry, would we have to spend equal time on all the good they do? Or could we specialize in the problems? I think it's very clear.

DAWKINS: I think Sam's asking more about—

HARRIS: Well, we could criticize Merck if they were especially egregious compared to some other company. If we were focusing on the pharmaceutical industry, not all pharmaceutical businesses would be culpable to the same degree.

DENNETT: Yes, right, well, so then the question is what? Is there something wrong with just—

DAWKINS: Sam's asking about whether we should be evenhanded in criticizing the different religions, and you're talking about evenhandedness regarding good versus bad.

HITCHENS: Whether all religions are equally bad.

DAWKINS: Yes, whether Islam is worse than Christianity.

HARRIS: It seems to me that we fail to enlist the friends we have on this subject when we balance this. It's a media tactic, and it's almost an ontological commitment of atheism, to say that all faith claims are in some sense equivalent. The media says the Muslims have their extremists and we have our extremists. There are jihadists in the Middle East and we have people killing abortion doctors. And that's just not an honest equation. The mayhem that's going on under the aegis of Islam just cannot be compared to the fact that we have two people a decade who kill abortionists. And this is one of the problems I have with the practice of atheism: it hobbles us when we have to seem to spread the light of criticism equally in all directions at all moments, whereas we could, on some questions, have a majority of religious people agree with us.

A majority of people in the United States clearly agree that the doctrine of martyrdom in Islam is appalling and not at all benign, and liable to get a lot of people killed, and that it is worthy of criticism. Likewise the doctrine that souls live in Petri dishes: even most Christians, 70 per cent of Americans, don't want to believe that, in light of the promise of embryonic stem-cell research. So it seems to me that once we focus on particulars, we have a real strength in numbers, and yet when we stand on the ramparts of atheism and say it's all bogus, we lose 90 per cent of our neighbours.

DAWKINS: Well, I'm sure that's right. On the other hand, my concern is actually not so much with the evils of religion as with whether it's true. And I really do care passionately about the fact of the matter: is there, as a matter of fact, a supernatural creator of this universe? And I really care about that bogus belief. And so, although I also care about the evils of religion, I am prepared to be evenhanded, because they all make this claim, it seems to me, equally.

HITCHENS: I would never give up the claim that all religions are equally false. And for that reason: because they're false in preferring faith to reason. And latently at least, they're equally dangerous.

DAWKINS: Equally false, but surely not quite equally dangerous. Because—

HITCHENS: No. Latently, I think so.

DAWKINS: Latently, maybe. Yes.

HITCHENS: Because of the surrender of the mind. The eagerness to discard the only thing we've got that makes us higher primates: the faculty of reason. That's always deadly.

DENNETT: I'm not sure that—

DAWKINS: It's *potentially* dangerous.

HITCHENS: The Amish can't hurt me, but they can sure hurt the people who live in their community if they have a little totalitarian system.

HARRIS: But not quite in the same way.

HITCHENS: The Dalai Lama claims to be a god king, a hereditary monarch, an inherited god, in essence. It's a most repulsive possible idea. And he runs a crummy little dictatorship in Dharamsala. And praises the nuclear tests. It's limited only by his own limited scope – the same evil is present.

HARRIS: But if you added jihad to that, you'd be more concerned.

HITCHENS: Well, look, every time I've ever debated with Islamists they've all said, 'You've just offended a billion Muslims,' as if they spoke for them. As if, and there's a definite threat to this, a menace, a military tone to what they say. In other words, if they'd said, 'You've just offended me as a Muslim,' that doesn't sound quite the same, does it? If they were the only one who believed in the prophet Mohammed. No, no, it's a billion. And, by the way, what's implied in that is, 'Watch out!' I don't care. If there was only one person who believed that the prophet Mohammed had been given dictation by the Archangel Gabriel, I'd still say what I was saying.

HARRIS: Right, but you wouldn't lie awake at night.

HITCHENS: And it would be just as dangerous that they believed that. Yes, it would. Because it could spread. The belief could become more general.

HARRIS: But in the case of Islam, it *has* spread, and it's spreading, and so its danger is not only potential but actual.

DAWKINS: Yes. I can see no contradiction. You're talking about different things.

HITCHENS: Yes, but over space and time, all that, I think, tremendously evens out. I mean, I didn't expect, and I'm sure neither did you, that in the sixties there would be such a threat from Jewish fundamentalism. Relatively small numbers, but in a very important place, a strategic place, in deciding to try and bring on the Messiah by stealing other people's land and trying to bring on the end. It's numerically extremely small, but the consequences that it's had have been absolutely calamitous. We didn't use to think actually that Judaism was a threat in that way at all, until the Zionist movement annexed the Messianic, or fused with it – because the Messianists didn't use to be Zionists, as you know. So you never know what's coming next.

HARRIS: Well, that I certainly agree with.

HITCHENS: And I agree that I'm not likely to have my throat cut at the supermarket by a Quaker. But the Quakers do say, 'We preach non-resistance to evil.'

That's as wicked as a position as you could possibly have.

HARRIS: Given the right context, yes.

HITCHENS: What could be more revolting than that? Saying you see evil and violence and cruelty and you don't fight it.

DENNETT: Yes, they're free riders.

HITCHENS: Yes. Read Franklin[1] on what the Quakers were like at the crucial moment, in Philadelphia, when there had to be a battle over freedom, and see why people despised them. I would have then said that Quakerism was actually quite a serious danger to the United States. So, it's a matter of space and time. But no, they're all equally rotten, false, dishonest, corrupt, humourless and dangerous, in the last analysis.

HARRIS: There's one point you made here that I think we should say a little more about, which is that you can never quite anticipate the danger of unreason. When your mode of interacting with others and the universe is to affirm truths you're in no position to affirm, the liabilities of that are potentially infinite. To take a case that I raised a moment ago, stem-cell research, you don't know in advance that the idea that the soul enters

[1] Benjamin Franklin (1706–90): leading figure of the American Enlightenment and one of the Founding Fathers of the United States; member of the Committee of Five that drafted the Declaration of Independence in 1776; President of Pennsylvania, 1785–8.

the zygote at the moment of conception will turn out to be a dangerous idea. It seems totally benign, until you invent something like stem-cell research, where it stands in the way of incredibly promising, life-saving research. You can almost never foresee how many lives dogmatism is going to cost, because its conflicts with reality just erupt.

HITCHENS: Well, that's why I think the moment where everything went wrong is the moment when the Jewish Hellenists were defeated by the Jewish Messianists – the celebration now benignly known as Hanukkah. That's where the human race took its worst turn. A few people re-established the animal sacrifices, the circumcision and the cult of Yahweh over Hellenism and philosophy. And Christianity's a plagiarism of that. Christianity would never have happened if that hadn't happened and nor would Islam. I have no doubt there would have been other crazed cults and so forth, but there might have been a chance to not destroy Hellenistic civilization.

HARRIS: You'd still have the Dalai Lama to worry about.

HITCHENS: Well, it's not a matter of numbers, it's a matter of, if I may say so, memes and infections. I would have certainly said in the 1930s that the Catholic Church was the most deadly organization, because of its alliance with fascism, which was explicit and open and sordid. Much the most dangerous church. But

I would not now say that the Pope is the most dangerous of the religious authorities. No question that Islam
is the most dangerous religion, and probably because it
doesn't have a papacy that can tell it to stop something,
make an edict saying—

HARRIS: Yes. No top-down control.

HITCHENS: By all means, yes. But I would still have to
say that Judaism is the root of the problem.

HARRIS: Although it's only the root of the problem
in light of the Muslim fixation on that land. If the
Muslims didn't care about Palestine, we could have
the settlers trying to usher in the Messiah all they
want. There would have been no issue. It's only the
conflict of claims on that real estate. Both sides are at
fault, but the only reason why 200,000 settlers could
potentially precipitate a global conflict is because there
are a billion people who really care whether those settlers tear down the Al-Aqsa mosque and—

HITCHENS: Which it's their dream to do. Because they
have the belief that one part of the globe is holier than
another – than which no belief could be more insane or
irrational or indecent. And so just a few of them, hold-
ing that view and having the power to make it real, is
enough to risk a civilizational conflict, which civilization could lose. I think we'll be very lucky if we get
through this conflict without a nuclear exchange.

HARRIS: That leads us to a very good topic. What are our most grandiose hopes and fears here? What do you think could be accomplished in the lifetime of our children? What do you think the stakes actually are?

DENNETT: And how would you get there?

HARRIS: And is there something we could engineer, apart from mere criticism? Are there practical steps? With a billion dollars, what could we do to effect some significant change of ideas?

HITCHENS: I feel myself on the losing side politically and on the winning side intellectually.

DENNETT: You don't see anything to do?

HITCHENS: In the current zeitgeist, I don't think we would be accused of undue conceit if we said of ourselves, or didn't mind it being said of us, that we've been opening and carrying forward and largely winning an argument that's been neglected for too long. And that's certainly true in the United States and Britain at this moment, it seems to me. But in global terms I think we're absolutely in a tiny, dwindling minority that's going to be defeated by the forces of theocracy.

HARRIS: So you're betting against us?

HITCHENS: I think they're going to end up by destroying civilization. I've long thought so. But not without a struggle.

DENNETT: Well, of course you may be right, because it can be a single catastrophe.

HITCHENS: That's my big disagreement with Professor Dawkins: I think it's us, plus the 82nd Airborne and the 101st,[1] who are the real fighters for secularism at the moment, the ones who are really fighting the main enemy. And I think probably, among secularists, that must be considered the most eccentric position you could possibly hold. That's tooth-fairy belief among those people. I believe it to be an absolute fact. It's only because of the willingness of the United States to combat and confront theocracy that we have a chance of beating it. Our arguments are absolutely of no relevance.

HARRIS: You may have many more takers, although not on the territory of Iraq. I mean, it may be that we need the 82nd Airborne to fight a different war in a different place, for the stated purpose.

HITCHENS: *Voilà!* By all means, there are reservations to be expressed by me, which I'll happily give you. But in principle, I think that's a very important recognition.

DAWKINS: Unfortunately we're running out of time.

HITCHENS: And possibly tape. [*Laughter*]

---

[1] Airborne infantry divisions of the US Army, specializing in air assault operations; active in Iraq and Afghanistan.

DAWKINS: I think we've had a wonderful discussion.

DENNETT: Yes, great.

DAWKINS: Thank you very much.

DENNETT: We've got a lot to think about.

ACKNOWLEDGEMENTS

The Richard Dawkins Foundation for Reason and Science, a division of the Center for Inquiry, expresses its deep gratitude for the generous contributions of Richard Dawkins, Daniel Dennett, Stephen Fry, Sam Harris, the late Christopher Hitchens and his widow, Carol Blue, to the making of this book.

This endeavour benefited from having the best professionals in the field guide its publication. John Brockman and his tremendous team at Brockman, Inc., including Max Brockman, Russell Weinberger and Michael Healey, supported the project from idea to fruition, and enlisted publishers around the world to bring it to life. Two top editors, Hilary Redmon of Penguin Random House US and Susanna Wadeson of Penguin Random House UK, greatly influenced the book's development and design, and were delightful to work with.

A special thank you to Sara Lippincott for her eagle-eyed and skilled copyediting, and her expert work finalizing a transcript that was challenging at best. And another to Gillian Somerscales, for her additional exacting copyediting and clarifying comments. We appreciate the assistance of CFI intern Andy Ngo.

We also wish to acknowledge the extraordinary contributions of the Four Horsemen, as well as the remarkable

Stephen Fry, to the vital cause of reason and science. They have changed the world for the better.

Robyn E. Blumner
President and CEO, Center for Inquiry
Executive Director, Richard Dawkins Foundation
for Reason and Science

Richard Dawkins is a Fellow of both the Royal Society and the Royal
Society of Literature and the recipient of numerous honours and
awards. He is also a Fellow of New College, Oxford. His first book.
The Selfish Gene, was voted the Royal Society's Most Inspiring Science
Book of All Time in 2017. He has since written a string of prestigious
books including *The Blind Watchmaker*, *Climbing Mount Improbable*,
The Ancestor's Tale, *The God Delusion*, two volumes of autobiography –
An Appetite for Wonder (2013) and *Brief Candle in the Dark* (2015)
– and, most recently, the anthology *Science in the Soul*.

Daniel C. Dennett is University Professor and Austin B. Fletcher
Professor of Philosophy at Tufts University. He is the author of
numerous books including *Intuition Pumps and Other Tools for
Thinking*, *Breaking the Spell*, *Darwin's Dangerous Idea*,
and *Consciousness Explained*.